REVOLT IN THE TROPICS

REVOLT IN THE TROPICS

Travels in the Caribbean

by

KARL ESKELUND

ALVIN REDMAN
LONDON

Published by
ALVIN REDMAN LIMITED
2 Clement's Inn, Strand,
London W.C.2
1963

PRINTED IN GREAT BRITAIN BY
BRISTOL TYPESETTING CO. LTD.
BARTON MANOR - ST. PHILIPS
BRISTOL 2

CONTENTS

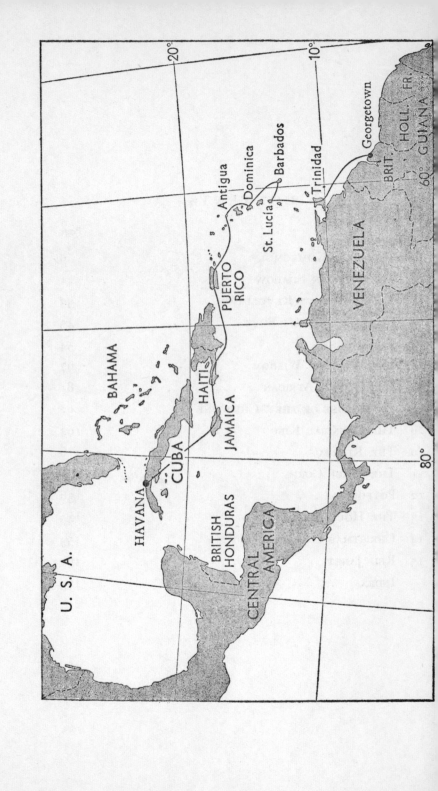

ILLUSTRATIONS

1 It seems nice that posters have disappeared in Cuba—but they have been replaced by portraits of Fidel Castro.

2 The young Cuban girls have joined the national militia with enthusiasm. This girl is an assistant in a shop in Havana's main street—she sells scent with her pistol in her belt.

3 Juan was somewhat better situated than before the revolution—if only the revolutionaries would let him have the deeds of the land he would find things very satisfactory. Until this became a reality you could not really tell their intentions.

4 "Today we are Socialists—tomorrow Communists!" cried these little fellows, raising their fists.

5 A bungalow at one of the new national farms. Ramirez, the farmer, facing the photographer, unfortunately Chi-yun covers the face of his wife. Today Cuba has more than 250 new national farms and about 600 co-operative ones.

6 The Ras Tafari Brothers show a dignity which is not usual among the West Indian negroes. Unconsciously they hope to find in Africa the soul which the black man lost when he was separated from his own culture.

7 The cabin on board *Christine*. Right : the two Americans who, in their hearts, did not actually approve of the way their fellow-countrymen treat the negroes.

8 "The Citadel" on top of a Haitian mountain. King Christophe built this proud castle hoping to be able to stand up to Napoleon from this position.

9 From our visit to the Caribs on the island of Dominica. This young girl removed the top with her teeth when I offered her a bottle.

10 Visiting the Redlegs in Barbados. The bright glare disclosed running sores on all legs and arms. It is Mrs. Gibson behind the children.

11 Pundit Sadhu was formerly a poor agricultural labourer. Since he made his way as spiritual adviser and faith-healer he has become a rich man.

12 The soil of many of the Caribbean islands is fertile, but the only tool known by the uneducated farmers is a hoe. The standard of living is very poor—in Haiti where this photo was taken the average annual income is less than twenty pounds.

13 Trinidad has an extremely mixed population, but the negro blood predominates.

14 Christmas in Trinidad's "shanty town". Some of the guests hid a broadsword beneath their clothes. When the dancing started they stripped to the skin.

15 Cheddi Jagan explaining his ideas to Chi-yun. "I am a Marxist," he said. He feels convinced that the best way of solving the problems of the undeveloped countries will be planned economy. Cheddi Jagan is a great admirer of Castro, but would prefer to use democratic means when carrying through his "revolution" in Guiana. However, much seems to indicate that the opposition will not allow this.

16 During the years of slavery family feeling was systematically killed among the negroes. The children grow up without traditions and without any kind of discipline.

CHAPTER ONE

CARIBBEAN KOMSOMOL

" PLEASE FASTEN YOUR seat belts. We'll be landing in a few minutes . . ."

My wife and I flattened our noses against the window for our first view of Havana from the air. On our only previous visit here five years ago we had arrived by sea.

The city lay stretched along the seashore : a colossus whose head spewed black clouds towards us from the oil refineries at the eastern end of the capital. They were followed by old Havana, looking just like a Spanish town with its church spires, narrow alleyways and wide plazas. Then came the new section, a little Chicago with arrogant skyscrapers. Finally we caught a glimpse of the luxurious residential quarters further west : snow-white villas along broad boulevards lined with palm trees.

The plane landed and we stepped out into the burning sun—to be greeted by tender words of love. They came from three colourfully dressed guitar players who were serenading us at the foot of the steps.

I was about to make a remark about the charming welcome, when we heard a loud, rasping voice coming from the hall for departing passengers. There, a long row of people were waiting to leave on our plane.

9

" Those who desert the fatherland in its hour of need are traitors," the voice shouted through a loudspeaker. " But the new Cuba can manage without these parasitic worms! We will continue to struggle without them! Long live our Socialist revolution . . ."

So this was the last farewell to Cubans going into voluntary exile. We glanced at the musicians who were still strumming their guitars. Their song of welcome had lost some of its charm.

We had expected to be cross-examined about the reason for our visit, where we were going to live, and so on, but not a single question was asked. A teenage soldier took our foreign currency and gave us Cuban pesos instead. That was to prevent us from changing money on the black market where we could have got five or six times the official rate. Another downy youngster in uniform stamped our passports, and then—Havana was ours.

On our first visit, we had been scared stiff whenever we took a taxi. Then, Havana had relatively more motor accidents than any other city in the world. All the drivers raced each other; but the revolution seemed to have had a restraining influence on them. The cab driver who took us to town kept well below sixty m.p.h. and we did not notice anyone going faster than that.

The commercial advertisements on the billboards along the highway had been replaced by patriotic slogans, some of them not without humour. " Cuba—the first liberated territory in the New World," we read. " If the North Americans don't like having a Socialist state ninety miles away—let them move !"

We noticed that the asphalt was covered by a layer of grease which had not been there before. That was from the exhaust,

our chauffeur explained. One finds it in all countries which
—like Cuba—use Russian petrol. I suppose it is due to poor
refining, for the raw product can hardly be so different from
that which is pumped out of the earth in capitalist countries.

Entering the town, we saw the first one of the long queues
which today are part of the street scene in Havana. What
were they waiting to buy?

Food, the driver replied. He added that virtually all foodstuffs were rationed. It seems that all roads to the promised
Socialist paradise are paved with shortages.

We went to the same place where we had stayed during
our last visit : a cosy hotel in the old section of the town. In
the hall, the picture of Batista, the former dictator, had been
replaced by one of Fidel Castro. Most of the rooms were
vacant. There were no tourists any more, the manager told
us—only an occasional ship with East German or Czech
labour heroes, and they lived on board.

When we lunched at a famous restaurant, the waiter
handed us a long menu, but as soon as we began to order
he informed us that only three dishes were served. Due to
rationing, they could not offer a wider choice. They had
not been able to get any meat that day, but if we wanted
to he could open a tin of pork imported from China.

" China !" my Chinese wife repeated indignantly. But her
country was on the verge of famine. Every month she sent
home a parcel with Danish ham and milk powder to her
hungry relatives. And meanwhile, China was exporting pork
to Cuba !

During a short stay in Jamaica on our way here we had
met a Cuban refugee, a *divorcée* whose mother and daughter
were still living in Havana. She had asked us to look them

up, and in the late afternoon we walked to their place which was only about a mile from the hotel. Everywhere we saw young people in uniform. Many of them smiled and waved to us. This pleased me so much that I began to lecture my wife about the innate kindness of the Cubans. They have none of the arrogance of the Spaniard, nor are they as morose and introverted as many Red Indians. Perhaps this is because nearly a third of Cuba's seven million inhabitants are negroes. Their indomitable *joie de vivre* and optimism seem to have left their mark on the whole people . . .

I got no further, for I had suddenly noticed that many of the young people greeted me by raising a clenched fist. A suspicion flashed through my mind—a suspicion which was later confirmed. They took me for a comrade from Czechoslovakia or Poland or one of the other Iron Curtain countries which have sent technicians to Cuba!

When we stopped in front of a queue and I took out my camera, a militiaman immediately came over. He was not smiling. It was strictly prohibited to photograph queues, he informed me. But why? Because such pictures would make people abroad believe that there was a food shortage in Cuba.

But so there was, said a voice from the queue. Otherwise they wouldn't be standing there. Someone else added that in the old days there had been plenty of everything, and several others chimed in.

Suddenly I felt very happy. In China, which we had visited recently, no one talks like that, and in Russia, where we were last year, only the youth have the courage to do so. Perhaps this revolution was different. Perhaps it did not follow the usual pattern which makes it treason to criticize.

The soldier took it surprisingly well. Yes, these were hard times, he admitted, but they must understand that a picture like that would be used by the enemies of Cuba—the North American imperialists, whose blockade was causing all the temporary shortages.

Some people in the queue nodded in agreement, but many seemed unconvinced. Now the soldier asked me if I was a "Checko." No, I was from Denmark . . .

Ah, Dinamarca! Several voices repeated the word. I felt proud that they knew of my country, but then someone said that Denmark was where she came from—or *he*—what was her name? Oh, yes, Christine Jorgensen!

Food shortage and blockade forgotten, they looked at me with sudden interest, as if hoping I could perform a similar transformation. As we walked on, with a final warning from the soldier never to photograph queues, their excited chatter followed us.

We passed some men playing chess on the sidewalk. They were so absorbed in the game that they hardly noticed when I photographed them. Several of them were negroes. During the following weeks we saw them every time we came by, even late at night. It had been a meeting place for the chess enthusiasts of Havana for many years.

The people whom we were to visit lived on the fourth floor of a modern apartment house. When we rang the bell, the door was cautiously opened a few inches and a female voice asked who we were. We began to explain that we brought greetings from Mrs. Jiminez . . .

The door was flung wide open by a young girl, behind whom stood a white-haired lady with spectacles. "Mrs. Jiminez is my mother," the girl said eagerly. "How is she . . ?"

"Shhhhh!" the old lady said, placing a finger to her lips. It was unwise to talk in the corridor, she continued, closing the door behind us. You never knew who was listening these days—especially not since those people had moved in next door . . .

" Oh, grandmother!" the girl interrupted. " You always think the worst of people! Why should they want to spy on us?"

The old lady explained that some weeks ago their former neighbour had left the country and a new family had moved in, a workman and his wife and children. How could they afford to live in such a flat, we asked? They really couldn't, the old lady replied, but nobody paid more than one-tenth of his wages in rent any more. As soon as anybody left the country, his flat would be taken over by a revolutionary worker, complete with furniture and all . . .

" I'm glad that some of the poor can get a decent place to live," the girl broke in, but her grandmother ignored her. This workman was a member of the local revolutionary vigilance committee, she continued. You found these committees all over the country. The members were supposed to keep an eye on people, that was why she was afraid . . .

" No, grandmother!" the girl said impatiently. " You misinterpret everything! All they do is to protect us against the counter-revolutionaries . . ."

Thank you very much, but she would rather do without their protection, the old lady declared, leading us into the living-room. The old-fashioned polished furniture contrasted strangely with a refrigerator in a corner. Many middle-class Latin Americans who own a Frigidaire think it a pity to hide it away in the kitchen.

My wife, who loves flowers, took a step towards a vase of dark-red roses to smell them. She stopped short—they were made of plastic, and this despite the fact that in Cuba you

14

can buy an armful of fresh flowers for next to nothing.

Instead of coffee we were served Coca-Cola. We chatted for a while about nothing in particular, but suddenly the antagonism which we had already sensed between the old lady and her grandchild erupted into the open. That was when we told them about Mrs. Jiminez' plans for the future. She intended to wait for them in Jamaica and hoped they would soon get permission to leave . . .

" There you are, Joan !" the old lady exclaimed. The sharpness in her voice surprised us. " You won't obey me," she continued, " but until you come of age you have to obey your mother !"

" I won't go away!" the girl shouted. " I'm a Cuban— I want to remain in my country !"

" What am I going to do with her?" the old lady asked, wringing her hands. " She has always been such a sweet and easy child, but after she joined the revolutionary youth club she has become impossible. They poison her mind with their propaganda !"

" Oh, grandmother, how can you say such a thing? They only teach us our duty to our country. Is that poisoning us?"

" You know very well what I mean. They tell you that there is no God and that you should only obey the State. Bring the book you use for teaching the maid—then they can see for themselves."

As soon as Joan had left the room the old lady turned towards us. " They are turning her into a Communist," she said. " That is why I want to get her out of the country."

Joan returned and handed us a booklet explaining that it was being used in the country-wide campaign against illiteracy. All the schools were closed for half a year so that the students could go out among the people and teach them to read and write. She herself taught their black maid at home.

" Fidel has sworn that before the end of the year there will not be a single illiterate left in Cuba," she told us with shining eyes. " Isn't that wonderful?"

As we leafed through the reader, our thoughts went back to a Soviet school we had visited the previous year. The English textbook used by the Russian children had contained the same glowing nationalism, the same glorification of the Socialist state.

Joan asked us if we were going to try to interview Fidel —Cubans never use his last name. Yes, of course, we replied. Oh, wouldn't we please take her along if we succeeded? Of course she saw him every time he appeared on television, but she wanted so much to meet him—that was her highest ambition.

" He will only fill you with lies," the old lady said bitterly. " Once I believed him, too, we all did, but now I know better."

Fidel never lied, Joan shouted. Oh, so he didn't, the grandmother exclaimed. Had he perhaps not promised free elections? Yes, Joan said, but how could you hold elections when Cuba was surrounded by enemies? There could be a new invasion any day.

He lied about other things too, the old lady continued doggedly. In every speech he promised that soon there would be an abundance of food, but the queues grew longer and longer. No one was starving, Joan retorted, and after a few months, when the new " people's farms " really started producing, there would be plenty to eat.

In a few months they would not be here any longer, the

It seems nice that posters have disappeared in Cuba – but they have been replaced by portraits of Fidel Castro.

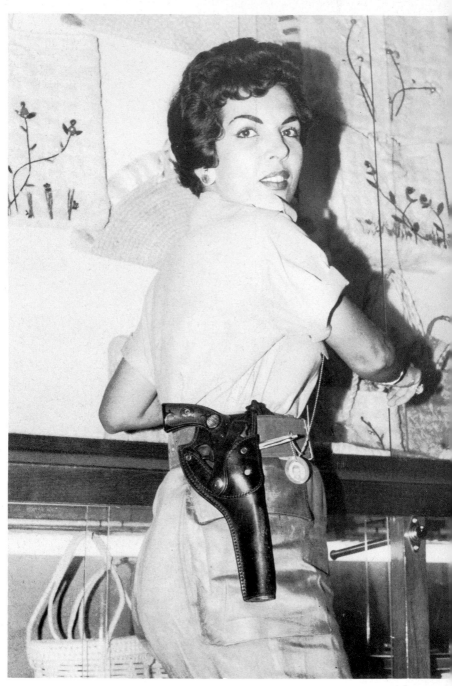

2. The young Cuban girls have joined the national militia with enthusiasm. This girl is an assistant in a shop in Havana's main street – she sells scent with her pistol in her belt.

3. Juan was somewhat better situated than before the revolution – if only the revolutionaries would let him have the deeds of the land he would find things very satisfactory. Until this became a reality you could not really tell their intentions.

4. "Today we are Socialists – tomorrow Communists!" cried these little fellows, raising their fists.

old lady said. Yes, they would, countered Joan defiantly—
she was going to stay, no one would force her to go to
Jamaica.

" It will be the death of me if you don't come with me,"
the old lady said brokenly. Then it would be her own fault,
Joan shouted and ran weeping from the room. Chi-yun and
I sat petrified. This unexpected scene had brought the revolution closer to us than all the political slogans we had
seen.

The old lady told us that their nerves had been on edge
ever since Joan's friends in the revolutionary youth club some
days ago had persuaded her to join the People's Militia. She
was convinced that if this happened, Joan would be entirely
out of her hands. Yet it was no use trying to prevent it, for
no one had any real authority over the children now except
the state.

Wasn't Joan too young to join? we asked. The grandmother said that she was only fifteen, but they took them
from the age of fourteen. The younger the better, because
then it was easier to make them believe in Fidel's lies. She
had tried to get the priest to talk her out of it, but Joan,
who used to be very religious, had called him an old reactionary and refused to listen to him.

At this moment Joan returned to the room without a trace
of tears. She was going to the revolutionary youth club, and
the old lady always accompanied her and then sat and waited
until she came out again. She would not let Joan go out
alone after dark.

" Of course not, that is improper for a young girl," the old
lady said.

" Not any more, grandmother. Everything has changed
since the revolution, but you are so old-fashioned."

It was almost dark when we came downstairs. We accompanied them to a building with pictures of Lenin and Castro over the entrance. Here they took their leave—a little old lady clutching the hand of a young girl who seemed to be straining to get away from her.

After dinner we went for a walk in the former amusement district in the old city. Five years ago, neon lights had turned night into day and exciting rhythms had blared from the open doors of the myriad night clubs. At that time, my wife had hardly dared to let me out of her sight, for the aggressive street girls had considered every male foreigner as legitimate prey.

Now the street were quiet and nearly dark and we saw only a couple of prostitutes who were standing outside a cheap hotel. From the opposite sidewalk, a young militiaman with a tommygun kept an eye on them. Professional girls had been permitted to continue their trade until the end of the year, and then that would be the end of that.

On every street, armed men were stationed about fifty or sixty yards apart. They were guarding against sabotage, as several large buildings had been blown up by the counter-revolutionaries. Once we heard shouts of command and saw a group of uniformed girls who were being taught to present arms. They did not look very warlike, for many of them had the well-developed bosoms and buttocks which one often finds among Latin women.

A passing car with a loudspeaker announced that a revolutionary dance would be held at eight o'clock at the *Habana Libre,* the American luxury hotel formerly called the Hilton. The best band in town would play and everyone was welcome.

We decided to go there and hailed the first taxi that came

along. After a short ride to the new section of the town we got off in front of the tallest and most modern-looking building in Havana. A stream of gay young people was already moving towards the entrance. They shouted jokes to each other and hummed a tune, but on reaching the hall they suddenly became silent. The thick rugs and opulent decorations seemed to make them uneasy.

" Imagine that all this is ours now," we heard a boy whisper to his girl. At the entrance to the ballroom the men had their pockets searched and the ladies their handbags. My wife had to open her compact to convince the guards that no explosives were hidden inside, but no one thought of examining my photobag which could easily have contained several pounds of dynamite.

The orchestra started just as we entered and in a few minutes the floor was crowded. Many of the white boys were in shirt sleeves, but we did not see a single negro without a jacket. It seems to me that those who come from the bottom rungs of society are often more afraid of breaking the conventions. There were hardly any " mixed " couples, and several times we saw white girls shake their heads when negroes asked them to dance.

The dancers did not use complicated steps but merely gave themselves up to the rhythm, nonchalant and relaxed. Soon perspiration was streaming down their laughing faces. When the first intermission came after an hour or so, one would have thought them ready for a rest, but someone immediately began to sing. A moment later they had formed a long conga line which wove through the room as they sang one verse after another, all about their beloved revolution. I remember one that went something like this:

Today we are all Socialists,
Tomorrow we will be Communists,
And if this progress makes you grieve
We will give you a laxative!

Their tramping feet made the floor shake. Even I began
to hum although I don't have an ear for music. Their enthusiasm seemed to me like a great force which would sweep
away all obstacles.

When the orchestra had started again I spotted a negro
dancing with a long cigar in his mouth. I hurried over and
asked him if I might take a picture of him and his partner.
First he wanted to know who I was and what I intended
to use it for. When I explained that I was a journalist he
took me aside and said there was something he wanted me
to write about. Would I please tell them " over there "—he
made a sweeping motion with his arm—that now the poor
were happy in Cuba, and especially the negroes. Before, it
had been impossible for a black man to go to a fine place
like this. All the good jobs had been reserved for the whites.
For the first time they had a government which treated them
as human beings and really tried to do something for all the
poor.

When I had photographed them, he put a big cigar into
my pocket and danced on. Shortly after that my wife and I
returned to our hotel. Passing through the hall, we glanced
up at the picture of Fidel Castro. We both felt that if anything sensible was to come out of all our bewildering first
impressions, it would be through understanding of him and
his background.

CHAPTER TWO

THE RUSSIAN SHADOW

ON ONE OF the first days after our arrival in Havana we looked up the Chief of the Information Bureau, a twenty-two-year-old revolutionary. He made a short speech to us, declaring that under the new government, oppression, exploitation, and poverty had been replaced by freedom, happiness and plenty. My wife and I were quite ready to believe every word of it, but we would have preferred to make the discovery ourselves.

When I offered him an American cigarette he shook his head and said: " Yanqui, no!" That is one of the revolutionary slogans against the North American imperialists. " Cuba, si!" he added when a secretary handed him a Cuban cigarette. A little smile would have changed the whole thing into a wisecrack, but he remained as solemn as an owl. I could not help thinking of China where the young revolutionaries also seem to have lost their sense of humour—something with which most Chinese are richly endowed.

We told the Chief that we were especially eager to learn something about agriculture and industry. Could he suggest how we should go about it? We expected him to overwhelm us with propaganda material and itineraries for visits to model collectives, but he simply replied casually that we had better go to ICAP—the Cuban Institute for Friendship among Peoples. They had more experience in assisting foreign visitors, he concluded.

ICAP had taken over a villa that had once belonged to a multi-millionaire, an absolute palace with marble floors, glittering chandeliers and antique French furniture. Among paintings of idyllic landscapes hung placards with excerpts from Fidel Castro's speeches: *Sweep away the worms. The unprivileged of yesterday are the privileged of today. In the new Cuba there are no bosses, only responsible comrades.*

The receptionist, a uniformed girl with a sub-machine-gun, asked us to sign the guest-book. We looked down the page. U.S.S.R., China, Czechoslovakia, Rumania, Bulgaria, Viet Minh . . . Most of the visitors seemed to come from the people's democracies.

While we were waiting we read the morning papers which lay on a table. There were three of them, but they were almost exactly alike except in name. The big news of the day was a Russian claim that the Soviet Union would soon overtake the imperialist nations in the economic race. " Communism will bring a happy future to all," a headline declared. Below was a drawing of a man reaching for a star on which was written : " Communism—the only solution to human problems."

There was also an interview with a female worker on a Soviet collective farm. Asked why she had volunteered to work overtime without pay, she declared : " To help produce more meat for the Soviet people, thereby strengthening our great fatherland in its struggle against the imperialists . . ."

" Please follow me," the receptionist said and led us to the director, a young man who did not look a day over twenty.

22

He welcomed us warmly and then asked which organization had sponsored our journey to Cuba.

Sponsored our journey? Yes, who had invited us? No one, we replied. His smile faded as he informed us that we had come to the wrong place. ICAP only looked after delegations with invitations from the government. We had better go to INIT.

That turned out to be a government travel bureau something like the Russian " Intourist." The revolutionaries must have established it in the hope that some day the stream of tourists will return to Cuba. Meanwhile, a whole army of cute office girls were trying to kill time in the huge office. They showered us with offers of cheap vacations at luxurious beach hotels. When we explained that we were more interested in agriculture and industry they advised us to go to INRA.

This is short for The Institute of Agrarian Reform, which is the main organization through which the revolutionaries run Cuba. With the exception of black market trade, all buying and selling goes through INRA, which controls all industries and collective farms, as well as railroads, buses and foreign trade.

Their headquarters is in a great new building on the outskirts of town. When we got there, close to a hundred people were standing or sitting in front of the entrance. Some, seemingly prepared for a long wait, were eating food which they had brought along.

Thanks to my press card we got past the heavily armed guards, and during the next hour or so we were sent from office to office. Uniformed boys and girls dashed about talking excitedly or dialling impatiently at telephones, apparently without ever getting an answer. Every once in a while we would see someone of our own age—we're in our early forties—wandering about with a lost expression. They wore civilian clothes; I suppose they were office workers inherited from the previous régime.

Every time we explained our errand, we were asked why we did not go to the information bureau, ICAP or INIT, and then sent on to another responsible comrade. When we were about to give up hope, a stroke of luck led us into the arms of a former journalist who immediately understood our problem. We were wasting our time here, he said.

Yes, I replied, we also had the impression that there was a little—er—confusion . . .

" Then you should have seen the place a year ago," he said with a grin. " This is nothing."

He did not want us to think that it was unwillingness to help that made everyone pass the buck. Everything was developing so rapidly in Cuba that it was impossible to keep track of it. If we wanted to find out what was going on we had better go out and collect our own information.

He hurried on. As we left, I felt a little annoyed that we had wasted a whole day running around in circles. This surprised my wife.

" Do you remember how furious you were in Red China and Russia because everything had to be arranged through the government?" she asked. " Here it is just the opposite— isn't that nice?"

" Yes," I replied and smiled, for she was right.

Early one morning a few days later we left Havana in a hired car and drove westward. During the first half-hour we must have passed a dozen motor-cars which had been left by the roadside. Some of them looked fairly new, but it was impossible to get spare parts now, so that when a car broke down it was often pushed to the side and abandoned.

As soon as we turned off the main highway we were in the real countryside. The farm cottages had roofs of straw which hung down over the mud walls like unkempt bangs. Here and there a lone royal palm rose high above the waving fields of sugar-cane. In the distance, foaming waves broke against a white beach, and inland we could see green mountains rising gently towards the blue sky.

" Lovelier land has never been seen by man," Columbus is supposed to have exclaimed the first time he saw Cuba. The elongated island, which is about the size of Denmark, Holland and Belgium put together, was then inhabited by an Indian tribe called *Siboney*. They were quiet, peaceful people who loved to lie in their hammocks (this is a Siboney word) and smoke tobacco (also from their vocabulary) which they inhaled through their nostrils.

The Spaniards discovered to their indignation that these natives were unacquainted with regular work. They did their best to teach them, but did not succeed. As soon as they began to use force, the Indians died off as quietly as they had lived. Only thirteen years after their conquest of the island, the Spaniards had to import the first negro slaves.

Hatuey, the chief of the Indians, was condemned to be burned to death. At the last moment a priest offered to baptize him so that he could go to heaven.

" Are there white men in heaven?" Hatuey asked. The priest nodded. " Then I do not want to become a Christian, for I do not care to go to a place where I will meet such cruel men."

Even the smallest bridges which we crossed were guarded by members of the people's militia. Some of them eyed us suspiciously, with a finger on the trigger. This made us uneasy, because we had heard what had recently happened to an Englishman who drove through the tunnel that goes under the entrance to the harbour of Havana. A sudden bang from the exhaust made the militiaman on duty think that a bomb had exploded, so he opened fire. The poor Englishman had to have six bullets removed from his back.

The landscape was already shimmering in the heat when, a little later in the morning, we saw black clouds rising from tall chimneys. That was an American sugar mill which had been nationalized, we were informed by a farmer creaking by in an ox-cart. As we approached, it grew into a whole town of bungalows grouped round some large buildings. An armed man stopped us at the gate and sent us on to the director's office.

" Come in !" a voice shouted when we knocked. A young man in shirt sleeves sat on the writing desk reading a newspaper, his legs dangling. Though he did not look fully grown he was puffing away at a cigar. Sorry, we said, it seemed that the director had not come yet.

" That's me," he informed us, jumping to the floor. We explained who we were and took out our identification papers, but they did not interest him in the least. We were welcome to see the sugar mill, he said, and shouted an order into the telephone. A moment later we were joined by a man who was old enough to be his father, Mr. Rodriguez, who was from the accounting department. He spoke English fluently and would accompany us as interpreter.

The mere thought of visiting a factory fills me with inexpressible gloom, but, thanks to the young director, it turned out to be rather an interesting experience. True, we did not learn much about sugar production from him. Every time we asked a technical question he would pass it on to Mr. Rodriguez. But he made up for this by giving us a clear and lively account of some of the factors leading up to the revolution.

As far as I remember it began by his accusing the United States of being a party to many of the crimes of the former Cuban dictators. Chi-yun and I looked questioningly at him. How was that possible?

He explained that the United States had dominated Cuban history ever since 1898. That was the year when the Cubans won their liberty from Spain after a long and bitter struggle which cost close to a quarter of a million lives and wrecked the economy of the island. The Spanish defeat was hastened by U.S.A.'s entry into the war. This the director admitted, and he praised the North Americans for their excellent rehabilitation work in Cuba.

But they would not withdraw their troops, he continued, raising his voice. Not until they had forced the Cubans to sign a treaty giving the North Americans the right to intervene with armed force whenever they deemed it necessary. The mere thought of this humiliation made him disgorge great clouds of smoke, like a volcano before an eruption.

" Do you realize what this meant?" he shouted. Some workers looked at us in surprise; apparently they were not used to seeing the boss so excited. " It meant that Washington had the final word in our affairs. The result was of course that our presidents really became errand boys of the North Americans."

But the presidents of Cuba had surely been elected by the Cubans, we countered.

He laughed contemptuously. There had been *one* honest election after the North American troops were withdrawn, he said—and then no more. The Yankees had left Cuba with an electoral system very much like their own. It was probably

27

suitable for disciplined Anglo-Saxons—but not for Cubans who had never known anything but the autocracy of the Spaniards. The presidential post became a prize which you either won by force or bought.

Already before the war of independence, the United States had large investments in Cuba. Now the North American capitalists got a free hand. They bought or bribed their way until they dominated the whole economy of the country.

" Do you realize that just about every sugar mill in the country belonged to North American banks?" the director asked. " They also owned about half the sugar plantations, most of the railroads, and nine-tenths of the power stations."

I later investigated these figures and they proved to be substantially correct. In those days Wall Street was the real master of Cuba, he continued, waving his cigar wildly. They could unmake a president if he did not suit them. Just a word from the U.S. State Department that intervention was contemplated, or a threat to buy less sugar, and he was through. But as long as he looked after the interests of the Americans he had nothing to worry about—and whether the Cubans liked him or not mattered very little.

Before President Roosevelt abrogated the treaty in the thirties, the United States had intervened three times. " Do you think they did it to protect democracy in Cuba?" the director asked. " No, on the contrary—every time they sent troops it was to help unpopular dictators protect North American property. All that interested them was that the dividends kept rolling in. As far as they were concerned, we Cubans could go to hell—and so we did!"

On the surface, Cuba had been an independent nation, he continued, but actually it was a North American colony. The Cuban upper classes had gone into the service of the Yankees.

28

They saw to it that Cuba produced the sugar needed by the United States—and nothing else. Though Cuba has some of the most fertile soil in the world, not enough food was produced for the Cubans. That was partly because the big plantations, which owned most of the land, let all soil not planted with sugar-cane lie fallow. By thus keeping labour plentiful they held wages down.

As a result, Cuba had to pay through the nose for industrial goods and foodstuffs imported from the United States. The agricultural workers could only find employment during the four months of the harvest. During the rest of the year they were left to fend for themselves. The economy of the country stagnated outside the short sugar season.

But fortunately all this belonged to the past, the director continued in a more gentle tone. The revolution had broken the vicious circle which had made it possible for the North American capitalists and the small Cuban upper class to exploit the poor. For the first time in history, Cuba was really independent. The sugar mills no longer worked for foreign investors, but for everyone. The farmers had been given land. Unemployment was fought by teaching them to raise crops which had formerly been imported and by starting new industries. The whole people took part in the rehabilitation work, their old lethargy replaced by enthusiasm, for they felt that now they finally had a government which did something for them . . .

We heard a hum of voices. It came from the lunch-room where fifty-odd men in work clothes were sitting in front of a woman who was teaching them to read and write. We had mentioned that we would like to talk to some workers, the director said. Here was our chance.

Such an interview is seldom satisfactory. What one seeks

29

is the personal contact which is usually lost in a crowd. With Mr. Rodriguez interpreting, I asked them a couple of questions about life before the revolution and now. It turned out that they received virtually the same wages as when the North Americans were running the sugar mill. The average was close to U.S. $5 a day for skilled labourers employed all the year round at the mill. The only change was that they no longer paid rent for their houses. This had formerly been from $7 to $10 a month. But now they had to pay for repairs and maintenance, so it actually came to about the same.

They could attend classes during their working hours because their comrades worked harder to make up for the lost time. Everyone was taking part in the campaign against illiteracy. They pointed to a large poster which showed how many were left in the district who could not read and write. Every week the number shrank.

When they had answered my questions the director suggested that we change roles. My wife and I had travelled extensively, and perhaps there was something that they would like to ask us?

After some hesitation, a middle-aged man cleared his throat and asked if we had been to the Soviet Union. We nodded. Was it true that workers there had their own cars?

No, I replied. We had visited several factories in Russia and many of the workers did not receive much more pay than they themselves did . . .

Suddenly Mr. Rodriguez stopped translating. The young director had risen from his chair. The Soviet Union must be the model for all socialist countries striving for a better future, he declared and thanked the teacher. For several minutes after we had left the room no one said anything. Then the director looked at his watch. Sorry, he said, but he had to attend a meeting. His colleague would show us the rest of the factory.

When he had gone I looked questioningly at Mr. Rodriguez. Had I offended the director? He shrugged and replied that Communists never liked to hear anything critical said about the Soviet Union.

So the director was a Communist? Yes, Mr. Rodriguez said, and so were most of the young people appointed to important positions these days.

At the entrance to the boiler-room we were stopped by an armed worker who would not let us pass until Mr. Rodriguez had explained who we were. We were told that during the past year there had been three serious cases of sabotage at the mill. Half a dozen workers had been arrested and, as far as he knew, two of them shot.

But why would the workers sabotage the revolutionary government? There could be several reasons, Mr. Rodriguez replied. Some were angry because the union leaders were now appointed by the government. Others were dissatisfied with the food shortage and the rising prices. Still others had friends or relatives among the approximately 200,000 political prisoners of the régime.

By questioning him some more we learned that for a while it had been difficult to keep the sugar mill running. First the whole North American staff had left, and then many of the Cuban technicians who were afraid that Castro would introduce Communism. There were really no trained people to replace them. The young revolutionaries appointed by the government had plenty of energy and enthusiasm, but this did not necessarily make up for their lack of experience. Nothing was run quite as efficiently as before and several times work had stopped because supplies did not reach the factory in time. Now they had a couple of Russian specialists who gave lessons to a selected group of skilled workers. Perhaps that would help.

On the way back to the office I asked Mr. Rodriguez if he had never thought of leaving. Yes, he replied—when he first heard rumours that all children were to be taken away from their parents and brought up by the State. That had fortunately proved to be untrue and now he was in a way glad to be taking part in the new experiment. He could not help admiring the young revolutionaries. They were very idealistic and not afraid to tackle even the most difficult problems. Perhaps they tried to do too much at once, but could one blame them for that? It had been bad in the old days when there was mass unemployment after the sugar harvest. Only the revolutionaries seemed to have the courage to try to change things.

"There hasn't been so much change here at the factory," Mr. Rodriguez said, as we got into the car. "But try to visit the farming country—things have really been happening there."

CHAPTER THREE

A TOPSY-TURVY REVOLUTION

WE LOOKED AROUND us in the bright and airy bungalow. A Danish farmer's wife would probably have felt it a bit cramped here, but would hardly have found much else to complain about. Besides the living-room, which measured nearly five paces in either direction, there were two tiny bedrooms, a small, fairly modern kitchen and a bathroom with shower, washbasin and bidet. The rather simple furniture which went with the house was of plain wood and there were tiles on all the floors.

"And how did you live before the revolution?" I asked the man of the house who was sitting opposite us, his horny hands in his lap. His name was Ramirez and he was a plain, straightforward man in his late twenties, although he looked older. At the moment he seemed a little embarrassed by the presence of two foreigners who had suddenly invaded his home.

Ramirez got up and found a photograph in the chest of drawers. It showed him and his wife with their five children standing in front of a little hut with a roof made of palm leaves.

"That is our old house," he said. "There was only one room, and of course neither water nor electricity. The

B   33

earthen floor was always muddy in the rainy season."

At that time the tobacco plantation where he was still employed had belonged to a rich Cuban. Ramirez had not paid any rent—agricultural workers hardly ever did in Cuba —and had also been allotted a small piece of land for growing his own vegetables. After the revolution the plantation had been nationalized.

" One can hardly recognize it any more," he said, looking out of the window at the neat rows of bungalows. There were a couple of hundred of them, all more or less like his own. The school and the people's shop rose a little above the other buildings. The whole complex was laid out along broad asphalt roads and looked very attractive with the green tobacco fields in the background. Compared to the usual Cuban farm dwellings it was like a glimpse of a fair new world.

I could not help smiling at the thought of the origin of the Cuban people's farm. A Scandinavian diplomat in Havana had told me the story. One day about four years ago, some young men from Castro's new Ministry of Agriculture had called on him. They were going to organize collective farms throughout the country and wanted some information about the co-operatives in Scandinavia—that was where the movement had begun, wasn't it?

Yes, the diplomat replied, but wouldn't it be wiser for the government to send a delegation to Scandinavia to study the results obtained there? The Russians had done so, before starting their collective movement.

There was no time for that, replied the young men, nor did they think it necessary. If he would just give them some pamphlets they would manage . . .

And they had indeed achieved some impressive results.

A Topsy-Turvy Revolution

Nearly two hundred and fifty state farms more or less like the one where Ramirez was working and six hundred-odd co-operatives are spread out over Cuba today. Generally speaking, though, the co-ops are not nearly as modern as the state farms.

The answers came slowly when we asked Ramirez to tell us what the revolution had done for him. Like many farmers he was rather taciturn, at least when he was with strangers. Political or economic theories did not seem to interest him in the least, but we could tell that he felt grateful to the revolutionaries for what they had done for him.

There was one expression he used several times. That was " *tiempo muerte* "—the dead period. It had played a calamitous role in his life and in the lives of his ancestors, and its power has not yet been broken, either in Cuba or in the other sugar-producing countries.

The dead period is a product of the plantation system. One finds it in all single-crop areas, whether the crops be sugar, tobacco or coffee. In the harvest season everyone is frantically busy, but it only lasts for a few months and during the rest of the year work is scarce. When the agricultural labourer has no money, the storekeeper, the butcher and the cinema owner feel it. The whole economy suffers.

The revolutionaries have not succeeded in doing away with the dead period, but they have taken some of the sharpness out of its sting. Not for everyone, it is true, but at least for those who work on the people's farms and the co-operatives. I could not get hold of the exact figures, but would estimate this to cover about a third of Cuba's 500,000 agricultural workers.

What have the revolutionaries done to solve the unemployment problem? They have instituted new crops such as rice, vegetables and fruit. Pigs and chickens are also being raised, and on this farm they were going to build a cigar factory. Why have cigars rolled in town, when they themselves had plenty of time during the winter months? But thus far the factory had not gone beyond the planning stage.

The state farm was led by seven government-appointed directors and a chief director. They sought to distribute the available work in such a way that there was some left for the winter. It was also a great help that so many did service in the people's militia. At the moment, more than a fifth of the men at the farm were called up—they lived at the expense of the state, and were even paid on top of that.

As a result of all this, the dead season had been reduced from eight to about four months. Did Ramirez make more money now? He explained that before the revolution he had done contract work earning slightly over five hundred pesos in a season (a peso equals one U.S. dollar at the official exchange rate). After the harvest he had usually gone to town to look for work, but had seldom succeeded in finding any.

When the tobacco plantation was taken over by the State it had first been made into a co-operative with the members sharing the work. INRA had given each one a guaranteed minimum of nearly two pesos a day depending a little on how many children one had. The money had not been paid out to them, however, but given them in the form of credit at the people's store. If the co-operative suffered a loss, the government covered it. If there was a surplus, the members divided it at the end of the year.

"We never got much," Ramirez said with a wry smile. "One year there was nothing at all, and the next year we got about twenty pesos each." He could not understand how the former owner had managed to become so rich.

A Topsy-Turvy Revolution

After two years the co-operative had been changed into a state farm. This meant that the workers no longer had any responsibility for the production. They were employees of the State, paid by the hour. The wage scale varied slightly according to the type of work. The average was about forty cents.

Weren't there some who shirked on the job? A wrinkle appeared on Ramirez's forehead. Yes, some worked less hard than others. They tried to explain to them that it was wrong. And if that did not help? He shrugged. There was nothing else they could do.

How big was his yearly income now? He counted on his fingers while his lips moved soundlessly. " Nearly 950 pesos," he said proudly.

I thought of the factory workers whom we had talked to a few days ago. Their salaries were the same as before. In this respect, the Cuban revolution differs sharply from the Chinese and the Russian. In these two countries, the rulers have concentrated on improving conditions for the industrial workers while the farmers footed the bill. I have sometimes wondered why this was so, since the farmers were worse off and more in need of help.

The explanation is to be found in Marxist theory, which maintains that only industrial workers are true revolutionaries. Castro, on the other hand, is not bound by such dogmas and considers the agricultural workers the true sons of the revolution.

The Cuban revolutionaries know that the rulers of Russia and China are struggling with a seemingly permanent agricultural crisis. The leaders of the collectives are usually blamed for this, but the real reason is undoubtedly that the farmers dislike the system and therefore do not make an effort. The pace is set by the least diligent.

Castro's people are sure that this will not happen in Cuba. They say that the collective system has a much better chance here, since about a fourth of the Cuban peasants have never been farmers in the real sense of the word, but plantation workers.

The members of the people's farms and the co-operatives are drawn almost exclusively from this peasant proletariat. As they have never owned land, never even owned their own homes, it is expected that they will adjust themselves easily to a collective way of life. In contrast to farmers in other socialistic countries they had nothing to lose by the new arrangement —but a great deal to gain, especially since Castro has been extremely generous towards the collectives, which are his pets.

It is as yet difficult to say whether this hope of the revolutionaries is justified. According to Castro, tremendous progress is being made in the country as well as in the towns. In a recent television broadcast he said that in the capitalist world, production increases by three per cent a year, in the Socialist countries by ten per cent—but in Cuba by no less than thirteen!

In Havana and the other towns, people ask impatiently what is happening to the alleged abundance of agricultural products. The revolutionaries reply that the temporary shortage of foodstuffs in the towns is caused by the increased buying power of the country people. The farmers get an increasingly large share of the national product, they say.

And this is certainly true, but when after taking leave of Ramirez we went to see the people's store, we found most of the shelves empty. In the food department there were only some canned goods from Poland and China, and when we examined the clothing, we discovered that most of it was of Russian make. The garments were expensive and poor in quality.

My wife and I could not help wondering whether some of the advantages reaped by the poor from the revolution have not been outweighed by Cuba becoming tied to the Socialist bloc. In Havana we had met several businessmen whose shops had not yet been nationalized. They all complained of having to pay unreasonably high prices for everything imported from Russia or the " people's democracies." One hardware dealer told us that the same Czech meat-grinder which he had imported before the revolution now cost three times as much.

Before leaving the people's farm we met the director of the newly-established truck farming department, a twenty-one-year-old negro by the name of Orete. He offered to show us some production statistics, so we accompanied him to his office. He spoke in a much more free and easy manner than other coloured Cubans we had met. Most of them think of themselves first as negroes, then Cubans. With Orete it was the other way around, and I think this was because his experiences as a revolutionary had created a special bond between him and his country.

Many white Cubans claim that there had never been a colour problem in this country until Castro created it. I think this is misleading, although there is a grain of truth in it. The revolution has indeed created tension between blacks and whites—but that is because the revolutionaries tackle a formerly dormant problem.

Cuba had never known open racial discrimination the way it is found in the southern United States, but this did not mean that Cuban negroes were free to go everywhere they wanted. Many hotels and restaurants in Havana as well as in other cities did not serve coloured people. They knew this, so they stayed away.

In the country when there was a public dance, the hall would be divided down the middle with a rope. One side was for the whites, the other for the coloured.

It was also impossible for negroes to get good positions, and they were not employed by the banks or department stores.

Fidel Castro has changed all this. He may have wavered in his political career, but where the colour problem is concerned he has followed a straight course. In his student days he started a society against racial discrimination. When he fought in the mountains, negroes and whites in his little army ate at the same table and slept in the same tents or caves. This was revolutionary in itself, for although white Cubans seldom have strong prejudices against negroes they do not mix with them socially. This line is still there, and even the revolutionaries seldom cross it.

I have heard Cubans say that after the revolution it is almost better to be black than white, and there is something in it. If there is a black and a white candidate for the same post, the revolutionaries will probably choose the negro even though he may not have as good qualifications. In this way they are trying to build up the self-confidence of the negroes, and after being treated for centuries as a lower kind of being, this is often necessary.

But Orete was different. He seemed to possess a high degree of self-confidence. The son of a poor plantation worker, he had joined Castro's forces about a year before the end of the civil war. His enthusiasm for the revolutionary programme—especially the promise of justice for everyone—did not seem to have cooled. His eyes sparkled when he talked about the rehabilitation work among the farmers.

A Topsy-Turvy Revolution

" My father always thought that he would die in the same miserable hovel where he was born," he told us. " Now he lives in a fine house on another state farm, and he keeps marvelling at it. It has been a topsy-turvy revolution, he says—the sons have liberated their fathers!"

His laughter filled the room. We never did get to see any of the promised statistics—when he opened a drawer to look for them he found such a mess that he quickly closed it again, saying that we had better get our information from INRA.

We learned that he had left school at the age of thirteen and had been a plantation worker until he joined Castro. He was not afraid to admit that he had no special qualifications for raising vegetables.

" But we revolutionaries have discovered that the school of experience is better than any other," he said. This may be so, but the results can be disastrous too when you appoint people to jobs they know nothing about. In Havana we had heard of a revolutionary city boy who was made head of a new poultry farm with 50,000 baby chicks flown down from Canada.

What happened after that we learned from a European who had been detained for a month on suspicion of espionage. In prison he had met the chicken-farmer and heard his sad story. The Canadians had sent instructions on how much to feed the chicks and what the temperature should be in the brooders. There was a great shortage of chickens and eggs, so the young patriot had decided to speed up production by raising the heat in the brooders and giving them more food. Whether it was due to heat or indigestion he did not know, but in any case they all died, and now he was charged with sabotage against the people . . .

Before leaving Orete we told him that we would also like to

41

meet a farmer who did not belong to a collective. He told us of a nearby village where there were many peasants who now owned the land on which they had formerly worked as tenant farmers.

Later in the afternoon we stopped in front of the first of a long row of houses that lay along a dusty road. In a rocking chair on the open veranda sat a man in working clothes. He was in his early forties, unshaven, and turned out to be extremely hospitable. His name was Juan, and as soon as we had explained our errand he invited us into the living-room. Here the air was fresh and cool, for the walls of the house, which he had built with his own hands, did not reach all the way to the ceiling.

He called his wife in from the kitchen which was installed in a lean-to in the backyard. Shyly she wiped her hands with her apron and bade us welcome. On the wall, among pictures of saints and bearded revolutionary leaders, hung their wedding photograph. Juan had not changed much since then, but she had become smaller and thinner and wrinkled. And no wonder, for she had borne him thirteen children, of whom eleven were still living.

They insisted that we should stay for dinner, and while she and the two eldest daughters prepared the food we talked to Juan. He could not tell us how much land he owned, at least not in any unit of measurement familiar to us.

" But it has always been enough for me to earn the bread for my family and myself," he said.

Tobacco was the only crop he raised. Before the revolution, twenty-five per cent of the harvest had gone to the owner of the land. The bank, which advanced him money to help him through the dead period, had taken twelve per cent.

A Topsy-Turvy Revolution

Shortly after the revolution the land had been distributed among the tenant farmers. Each one got exactly as much as he used to rent. Landlords who had worked the land were allowed to keep as much as they themselves had tilled.

Today Juan paid only twelve per cent of the harvest to INRA as a kind of tax. The bank took three per cent.

In other words, now he paid a total of fifteen per cent as against thirty-seven per cent in the old days? Juan nodded. But that was surely a tremendous improvement for him? Again he nodded, but without any visible sign of enthusiasm.

The table was only set for Juan, his three eldest sons, Chi-yun and myself, and we did not succeed in persuading Juan's wife and the girls to sit with us. They preferred to eat after we had finished, they said. This seemed to be the custom when there were guests.

The food was good, though it contained too much starch for our taste. We had fried chicken and a big dish of brown beans, and in addition got rice, bread, potatoes, yams and a kind of pancake made of corn meal. When we told them that food was scarce in the towns, they replied in one voice that it was also scarce in the country. Everything had gone up in price since the revolution, and there were many things you could not get any more.

Only the price of tobacco had remained the same. Now they had to hand over the entire harvest to INRA, and, considering the high cost of living, they received far too little for their tobacco.

But their real income was higher than before the revolution, wasn't it?

They thought for a moment, then agreed that they were slightly better off than before.

43

And now the land was theirs, I added. That must mean a great deal to them.

But *was* it really his land? Juan asked, looking up. He was busy rolling some giant cigars which he was going to smoke in the field tomorrow—ten altogether: that was his daily consumption. True, the INRA people had *said* that it belonged to him, he continued, but they had never given him any written proof. He was not permitted to sell it if he wanted to, and if he died, only his eldest son could inherit it. All this worried him.

When we were drinking coffee, Chi-yun and I told them about our visit to the state farm. The workers there earned more than Juan, so wouldn't he like to become a member of such a farm?

No, definitely not, he replied—he preferred to work independently. If they would only give him a deed to the land he would be satisfied. Until then one could not be sure of their intentions . . .

When we left, the whole family came out on the veranda to wave goodbye to us. The last we saw of them was the glow of Juan's cigar in the darkness.

CHAPTER FOUR

CIGARS AND LITTLE BOYS

ON OUR JOURNEY through Cuba we would sometimes forget that we were in a country which was in the throes of a revolution. This was especially the case when we visited small provincial towns. A peaceful atmosphere reigned in the narrow alleys where donkeys' hooves still clattered on the cobblestones and young couples stole caresses through Spanish lattice windows in the evenings. The main street invariably led to a plaza where people dozed or talked in the shade of big trees. Havana, with all its change and activity, seemed far, far away.

We had expected that, with the exception of Havana, Cuba would be an underdeveloped country, but all the provincial towns had an air of prosperity seldom found in the Latin-American world. There were surprisingly many private cars and fine shops, although the selection of goods was now limited.

It is typical of all underdeveloped countries that the majority of the population are farmers—in India close to ninety per cent, in China around eighty. In Cuba, on the other hand, nearly sixty per cent of the people live in towns and the middle class is relatively larger than in any other Latin-American country. When Castro came to power, the living standard was approximately the same as in Italy.

There is one great difference between city and country, however : before Castro started his campaign against illiteracy, forty per cent of the rural population were unable to read and write against ten per cent of the city dwellers.

Some friends in Havana had assured us that we could get excellent food in the provinces. They had given us a list of the best restaurants, but it seemed as if we were following on the heels of a revolutionary nationalization commission. Everywhere we went, the good eating places had just been taken over by the government. Even so, we did not have to go hungry, but the standardized meals were definitely not inspiring.

At one place, we visited a cigar factory which had also been nationalized a short while ago. There were close to a hundred workers, mostly women, who earned between U.S. $85 and U.S. $120 a month—the same as before the revolution. The walls were covered with revolutionary slogans and the radio, which was turned on full blast, had mostly political programmes, but apart from that their lives had not changed very much. Some of them puffed away at big cigars while they worked—they were permitted to smoke five a day and chose the longest ones. They preferred not to be photographed with a cigar in the mouth, however. It looked unfeminine, they said.

Before the revolution, this factory had produced close to 2,000,000 cigars a day against a mere 50,000 today. The North Americans no longer bought Cuban goods, and Cuba's new customers in the Iron Curtain countries could not afford to import Havana cigars.

That they are relatively expensive is not surprising when one has seen how they are produced. Driving through the tobacco country we had passed huge, low tents that looked like those of the Bedouins. Here grew the wrapping leaves under nets of gauze which protected them against insects. This is a costly but necessary precaution : just a tiny hole in the leaf, and the cigar does not draw.

We were also permitted to enter one of the airtight underground storerooms where the tobacco is " ripened "—but hurried out again, gulping for air. The humid air was heavy with nicotine, and we were told that no one could stay down there for more than an hour at a time. The best tobacco is stored for about thirty years in such cellars.

It took time to produce a hand-rolled cigar. Their fastest worker, a pretty mulatto woman, could only make about a hundred a day. But a single one of the big, complicated machines could spew out more cigars in a couple of hours than even Churchill could smoke in a lifetime.

The middle-aged man who showed us around was chief of the hand-made cigar section. He told us that until the factory was nationalized it had belonged to him. The ex-owner now worked for one hundred and fifty pesos a month, or about a tenth of his former income.

Not many people would find this amusing if it had happened to themselves, but he smiled as he told us about it. At first it had been difficult for him and his wife to get used to living on so little.

" I must admit that we planned to go to Miami," he continued. " But then we thought of the empty life awaiting us as refugees in a foreign country, so when the revolutionaries offered me the job, I accepted. We have not regretted it. We are Cubans, and whatever happens, we prefer to remain in our own country."

Driving on after the visit to the cigar factory, we saw a

straggling column of militiamen cross a field and climb into waiting trucks. They had been out hunting counter-revolutionaries who were hiding in the mountains close by. It was strange to think that barely four years ago Castro had also fought from the mountains to overthrow a tyrant. Now his place had been taken by others who considered him a tyrant. History does repeat itself.

The counter-revolutionaries seem to have a rather extensive organization. Some days ago in Havana, a young shop assistant had taken me aside and asked if I wanted to contribute a little to the struggle against the Castro dictatorship. He was selling " freedom bonds," he said, showing me a bunch of coupons.

" Against Communist oppression," it said on one side under a drawing of a soldier blowing a bugle, and on the other : " The real revolution," and " For Cuba and Cuba's freedom." Each coupon was numbered; the one I bought for a peso had Number 26,222 on it.

" Be sure to hide it," the shop assistant said. His advice was superfluous, since I knew that the punishment for possessing a freedom bond was the same as for writing anti-Communist slogans on the walls : seven years' imprisonment.

The counter-revolutionaries use the same tactics as Castro did in his struggle against Batista : hit-and-run tactics on isolated groups of government troops and sabotage with bombs. During our stay in Havana we frequently heard explosions at night and every week several resistance fighters were executed, usually young people. But no mention appeared in the newspapers.

The counter-revolutionary movement probably does not have much chance unless it also receives support from outside—but the very threat of invasion is one source of Castro's

48

5. A bungalow at one of the new national farms. Ramirez, the farmer, facing the photographer, unfortunately Chi-yun covers the face of his wife.
Today Cuba has more than 250 new national farms and about 600 co-operative ones.

6. The Ras Tafari Brothers show a dignity which is not usual among the West Indian negroes. Unconsciously they hope to find in Africa the soul which the black man lost when he was separated from his own culture.

The cabin on board *Christine*. Right: the two Americans who, in their hearts, did not actually approve of the way their fellow-countrymen treat the negroes.

8. "The Citadel" on top of a Haitian mountain. King Christophe built this proud castle hoping to be able to stand up to Napoleon from this position.

strength. As in China and Soviet Russia, the revolution derives its power first of all from nationalism, which again thrives on the hatred of a common scapegoat : Yankee imperialism.

According to our acquaintances in Havana, Castro's popularity had reached an all-time low just before the attempted invasion in the summer of 1961—but rose immediately when Cuba was threatened from the outside.

When we stopped for lunch at a small provincial town, we got an inkling of how strong nationalism is among the young.

At our table sat two students with whom we got into conversation. They studied at the University of Havana, but at the moment were taking part in the campaign against illiteracy.

We asked them how conditions were now for the students. Excellent, they replied. Both came from lower middle-class homes and before the revolution their parents would probably not have been able to afford to pay for their studies. In any case Batista had closed the university during the last few years of his rule, well knowing that his opposition drew its main strength from there.

One of the first things Castro did was to re-open the university, and now studying was practically free of charge. Was the scholastic standard as high as before? Yes, they said. It was true that several liberal professors had gone into voluntary exile, and others had been dismissed because they were thought to be enemies of the régime. But the people who had replaced them were just as good, they thought. Among them were a couple of Russian professors who were already able to lecture in Spanish. They were highly respected.

Was there much attempt to influence the students politically? They hesitated a moment, then nodded. Everybody had to take a course explaining the Marxist-Leninist principles.

49

Did they think that Marxism was the best solution for Cuba? No, they replied, this time without hesitation. They would both prefer their country to follow the democratic tradition, but how was it possible to hold elections as long as the North Americans were plotting against Cuba? Both felt that Yankee intrigues had forced Castro to seek the aid of Russia. In their opinion, there was no other way out as long as the North Americans continued their aggressive policy.

Anyway, there was no reason to believe that the government would introduce real Communism, one of the boys said. (This was shortly before Castro announced that he was a Communist.) At nearby tables sat several military people, but he did not seem afraid of being overheard. " It wouldn't work well here," he continued. " Don't you agree?"

He turned to his friend, who nodded. We could feel that they would both rather change the subject, and during the rest of the meal we talked about other things.

In the afternoon, a couple of days later, we came to a town where banners with political slogans were strung across the main street, which was alive with people. What was going on? we asked a passer-by. He explained that in a little while there would be an anniversary parade in honour of a local revolutionary who had fallen in the struggle against Batista.

We had thought of driving on, but quickly changed our minds and found a room at a nearby hotel. When we returned to the street we heard rousing military music and a moment later the people's militia marched by, headed by a brass band. Behind them came a column of Pioneers from the revolutionary youth movement, followed by a couple of dozen boys who did not look more than five years of age. They were also in uniform, but hopelessly out of step. Alongside them marched an officer, chewing a cigar.

Cigars and Little Boys

When they were almost in front of us he took the cigar out of his mouth and shouted an order. Immediately the boys raised their tiny clenched fists and shouted something in chorus. At first I thought my ears had fooled me, but they repeated the slogan a moment later: " Today we are Socialists, tomorrow Communists!"

My wife and I remained standing there until the procession had passed. We did not say a word, and for a long time after the sound of the childish voices kept ringing in our ears.

In the evening, when we went out to eat, the foyer of the hotel was full of people sitting in rows and staring at a television screen above the reception counter. Fidel Castro was speaking—slowly and earnestly, his voice rising and falling like a preacher's. At the sight of him—bearded, with both arms raised above his head—we suddenly understood why many Cubans compare him to Jesus. There is more than an outward resemblance. He too had brought hope to the oppressed and given them a new belief.

But Castro's kingdom is of this world, and it was not love that he preached. Though we lingered only for a few minutes, twice we heard him raise his voice and attack the " Imperialists and capitalist exploiters " in North America.

While we were dining at a nearby restaurant an elderly, slightly tipsy man came over to our table and started talking to us—with a pronounced American accent. Our startled expressions made him smile. " Yes, I'm probably the last Yankee left in Cuba," he said. " All the others have run away."

We asked him to sit down and learned that he had been a Socialist from his early youth. Life in the capitalist United States had never appealed to him, so he had roamed the

51

world, making a living as a masseur. Shortly after the revolution he had settled in Cuba.

" I'm for Fidel," he said noisily, raising his glass. " Long live the revolution !"

People turned to look at us from the other tables. When we were going back to the hotel he insisted on accompanying us. As soon as we got out in the street he began singing another tune. He still believed in Socialism, he said. " But I'm fed up with the Fidelistas. This is not Socialism—it's anarchy !"

We stopped, surprised at the sudden change. What specifically did he have against the Cuban revolution? That they executed so many people and didn't hold elections, he replied, but without much conviction. Only when he got around to his more personal grievances did his voice begin to tremble with indignation.

The revolutionaries made a mess out of everything, he said. Although they insisted that production was rising, it had actually gone down during their rule. As a result, he had to do without most of the pleasures which an old man like him could still get out of life. It was impossible to get decent food any more, and the beer got worse and worse. He used to be fond of reading newspapers, but now they contained nothing but propaganda. Prices kept rising, and now he had been prohibited from renting out his two spare rooms.

But the worst thing was that the people's militia kept picking him up for questioning, usually during the night. They would keep him for hours, asking the same questions over and over again. He was convinced that they did this solely because he was an American. He had explained to them that he had been a Socialist before they were born, but that didn't help in the slightest.

" Every time those pups have nothing better to do they

come and arrest me," he said bitterly. " I wish I could get away from here, but I have put all my money in a small house, and now I'm not allowed to sell it."

Practically all the people he knew were now against the revolution, he said. " When Fidel talked a year or two ago, you could walk through town without missing a word—his voice came from every house. Now there aren't many who listen to him any more, and no wonder! He talks too much! Imagine, one of his speeches lasted over eight hours!"

We parted in front of our hotel. Though Castro had not yet finished speaking, several of the chairs in the hall were empty. A couple of those who still held out were dozing. We were about to go upstairs, when thunderous applause came over the loudspeaker. The picture on the screen had changed: instead of the revolutionary leader, we saw his audience in a tightly-packed hall. Most of them were in uniform, and practically all were extremely young.

" Izquierda!" they shouted, raising their left fists. " Fidel, izquierda, Fidel, izquierda!" (Fidel, lead us to the left!)

Again, Castro appeared on the screen. He beamed with satisfaction, raised his arms for silence, and resumed his speech.

CHAPTER FIVE

THE HORSE

DURING OUR STAY in Havana my wife and I turned into a couple of night owls. In a way Fidel was to blame for this for every time we stepped out late in the evening, it was really in the hope of meeting him.

We had requested an interview on our arrival, but a friendly man at the information bureau had told us that there was virtually no chance at all of getting to see him in this way. Not that Castro minded talking to foreign journalists. In fact, he liked it, but it was nearly impossible to get in touch with him, since he worked without a fixed schedule, simply following his inclination; even his secretaries had a difficult time keeping track of him.

But there were a couple of restaurants where he liked to go for a meal after his television appearances, which usually lasted until late at night. If we visited them frequently we could hardly help seeing him sooner or later, and then we should go over and introduce ourselves.

On one of our last evenings in Cuba we were sitting as usual in one of Castro's favourite restaurants waiting for him to appear. With us was a thirty-three-year-old Cuban doctor whom we had invited for dinner. The only other guests in the dining-room were a party of foreigners who, judging by

the width of their trousers, came from one of the Iron Curtain countries. The occasional snatches of conversation which
reached our ears sounded like Russian. The waiters were
yawning, probably hoping that soon we would all go home.

But we had emptied a couple of bottles of wine and were
talking away—of course, about the revolution and Fidel
Castro. Few Cubans believed that he was a Communist, but
why had he declared war on Cuba's middle-class? This question was very much on our minds.

The doctor was of the same age as Castro and knew him
slightly from his university days. He told us that Castro was
the son of a Spanish emigrant who, through hard work, had
become the owner of a large cattle ranch. He remembered
Castro, who is now a heavyweight of some fifteen stone, as a
tall, skinny and intense young man with rapidly blinking eyes
enlarged by thick glasses. Though still extremely near-sighted,
he now refuses to wear glasses—they look laughable on a
leader, he says.

" Many people get the impression that he avoids looking
them in the eye," the doctor said. " But that may be due to
his weak eyesight."

The students called him " *El Caballo* "—The Horse—and
this is still his most popular nickname. Then, as now, he
dressed sloppily and was invariably late for appointments. He
studied law and like the great majority of Latin-American
students was influenced by Leftist ideas.

" But he kept away from the Communists. He was too much
of an individualist to join any party—he could never have
stood the discipline. We thought of him more or less as a
Liberal of the Roosevelt school."

The doctor explained that at that time the Communists
were in the doghouse among Cuban intellectuals for sup-

porting the dictator, Batista, during an election a few years previously. Batista was an army stenographer who, when he first seized power in the middle thirties, had with one stroke promoted himself from sergeant to colonel. From then on he and his cronies had run Cuba as a private business. Those who protested were beaten up or murdered by his police.

Though respected by the other students for his quick mind and his gift of oratory, young Fidel was never near the top of his class, perhaps because he spent so much of his time agitating against the dictatorship. Whenever there was a demonstration, you were sure to find him at the head of it. He still has a small scar on his forehead caused by a blow from a police truncheon, and twice he had to go into exile for short periods to avoid arrest.

" He never lacked courage," the doctor said, and smiled. " Once he participated in an expedition against Trujillo (the then dictator of the Dominican Republic). A Cuban gunboat stopped the invasion fleet and arrested all the participants except Fidel, who jumped overboard and swam three miles to the shore."

In 1953, Fidel Castro passed his final exams as a lawyer. Just before this, he had married a beautiful society girl who bore him a son. Politics attracted him more than family life or his new and not too successful practice, however, so that when a congressional election was scheduled he put himself up as a candidate. That was during a period when Batista was " out."

But before the election Batista again seized power by a coup—and Castro saw his own political career nipped in the bud. The other candidates shrugged their shoulders, but Castro decided to fight back. He became leader of a band of nearly two hundred revolutionaries who, early one morning, attempted to capture an armed fortress and a radio station in Santiago, the second largest city in Cuba.

" It was madness," the doctor said. " Fidel expected that the moment he announced the capture of the fortress over the radio, all Cuba would join the revolt. He has always been a visionary."

The rebels, fleeing after a short struggle, were surrounded on a steep mountainside and then murdered as hunger and thirst forced them to surrender. Only Fidel, his brother Raul and thirty-six others were spared—not through mercy, but because news of the butchery created a wave of indignation. Hundreds of prominent citizens sent protests to Batista, and this caused him to rescind his order to kill all the rebels.

" I doubt whether any similar protest today would make Castro spare one of his opponents," the doctor added. Probably not, I agreed, thinking of a report I had read by two American leftist economists who had spent an evening with Castro. When they met him, he seemed extremely depressed. Asked what was wrong, he told them about two of his former men who had joined the counter-revolutionaries. They were caught and condemned to long prison terms, but had now escaped from prison.

" And when they are recaptured we have to shoot them," Castro concluded. " That is what makes me so sad."

Batista promised to give the surviving rebels an open trial, but broke his word when the turn came to their leader. Preliminary investigations had made it clear that if the eloquent young revolutionary got a chance to speak he would win the sympathy of the public.

So Castro was declared ill and sentenced behind closed doors. Conducting his own defence, he made what the doctor considered the most inspiring speech of his life. Of course it was not made public, but someone present at the trial had taken it down in shorthand. Today, some young revolutionaries know whole pages of it by heart.

From Castro's opening words it seemed as if it was not he but the Batista régime that was on trial. Had not Batista violated the constitution by seizing power without an election? The rebels as enforcers of the law had only done their duty by attempting to overthrow the dictator.

The revolutionaries were bound to win in the end because they had the people on their side, the prisoner continued. By *the people* he did not mean the conservative elements which supported any régime that protected their privileges, but the masses to whom all made promises and whom all deceived.

He was condemned to fourteen years' imprisonment. While in jail he was divorced by his wife, who then married a man connected with the Batista government. This probably increased Fidel's bitterness towards the upper class, the doctor said.

After a year and a half, Batista felt so sure of his power that he decided to pardon the Castro brothers. All he required was Fidel's promise not to make another insurrection attempt. Nothing doing, Fidel Castro replied from prison where he was busy teaching his fellow prisoners revolutionary tactics. Batista finally released him unconditionally.

Together with Raul he went to Mexico, where they immediately began to prepare for a new revolt. About two years later they returned to Cuba in a motor boat together with eighty-two other revolutionaries, toughened by months of training in guerilla warfare.

Though Batista had an army of 40,000 men, Castro was

convinced that he could overthrow him in a few days. His plan called for demonstrations in several towns simultaneously with the landing of the invasion force. The people, inspired by the news that the struggle for freedom had commenced, would immediately rise against the dictator . . .

" Exactly the same naïve optimism as he had shown during his first attempt to seize power," the doctor remarked, shaking his head. " And it turned out just as badly this time."

Everything seemed to have conspired against the little band of rebels. A storm drove the boat out of its course. The demonstrations fizzled out, and when the revolutionaries finally landed, half dead from seasickness, they were quickly located by Batista's forces. A merciless chase began. A week later, when the survivors met in an almost inaccessible mountain district not far from Castro's childhood home, only thirteen were left.

Castro's greatest assets are his incredible stubbornness and his perseverance, the doctor continued. When the remnants of the defeated invasion force huddled together in a cave the first evening, frozen and hungry, he made a long speech to them, starting with the words : " Victory is now within our reach . . ."

Batista announced that the entire invasion force had been wiped out. Somehow, Castro had to let the Cuban people know that he was still alive. This he did by letting an agent in Havana promise *The New York Times* an exclusive interview if they would send a correspondent up to him in the mountains.

The journalist was probably delighted when the rebels blindfolded him for the last few miles of his journey to their hideout : this added drama to his story. Castro talked to him throughout a whole night, and his unshakable confidence in final victory made a great impression on the American correspondent.

"I still remember what a stir it created in Cuba when the story was published," the doctor went on. "There was an aura of romance about the indomitable rebels in the mountains. Everybody talked about them, and during the next couple of years, droves of journalists went up to see Fidel."

Others came too. Little groups of Cubans who were against the dictatorship sneaked out to the mountains and joined the revolutionaries. Cubans in the United States started a collection for them and bought arms, medicine and food which were smuggled up to them. Fidel Castro also got a radio transmitter.

"I think the transmitter contributed more than the arms did to his winning the war—if you can call it a war," the doctor said. "No more than six hundred men fell on both sides, and Batista was never really defeated in the military sense."

Castro was still convinced that he could win through an insurrection which was to start with strikes in the towns. When victory finally came, however, it was in quite a different way.

The mountain hideout of the revolutionaries slowly grew into a regular base with a small landing strip and a primitive hospital. Apart from tutoring the children of the neighbourhood, who had never had a chance to go to school, the revolutionaries were not very active. But every night the nation would listen to the voice from the mountains and exult. David was defying Goliath! Castro always concluded his broadcasts, which often lasted half the night, with a promise of free elections once a victory had been won.

The Horse

In the spring of 1958 Batista sent 9,000 men against the rebels, but the professional soldiers, who knew nothing about guerilla warfare, withdrew in disorder after snipers had killed off a few of them.

Encouraged by this success, Castro announced over his radio that the hour of freedom was at hand and ordered the workers of Cuba to go on strike. He believed that when the army realized that the whole country was against Batista it too would turn against the dictator. Then he and his revolutionaries, who now counted over a thousand, would come down from the mountains and take over.

But the strike failed, partly because the Communists, who had great influence within the trade unions, did not trust Castro. They told their people to go to work as usual. In the doctor's opinion, there was another and even more important reason why Castro's " order " was disregarded. Generally speaking, the workers were not dissatisfied with Batista. There had been considerable economic progress under the dictatorship, especially in the towns. The bearded Robin Hoods in the mountains appealed to the imagination of the people, but few took them seriously.

" In other words, Fidel was let down by his beloved people," the doctor continued dryly. " In fact, during his difficult years in the mountains, only the middle-class which he despises so much gave him active support. It was our money which purchased his supplies, our young people who joined his army. We—and *not* the workers and farmers—were willing to make sacrifices in the struggle for freedom."

After the unsuccessful strike, Fidel decided in desperation to step up rebel sabotage which had already been going on for some months. His people sneaked down from the mountains and set fire to the sugar cane fields, blew up gas and

61

power plants, and threw bombs at members of Batista's police force.

Batista could not strike back, for his enemy was invisible. His henchmen in turn stepped up their campaign of terror against the middle-class, whom they knew were supporting Castro. Thousands of suspects were beaten mercilessly or thrown into jail. The students suffered most of all. Every day young men were killed or tortured.

Batista's men could hardly have done anything more stupid, for the students are much respected in all the Latin American countries. Even the army, from which Batista drew his main support, began to grumble.

In the autumn of 1958 Castro sent two columns of a couple of hundred men each down from the mountains. To their own surprise they were able to advance practically without meeting any resistance. The army avoided battle, and at the first large provincial town which the rebels reached they were received like heroes.

A few days later Batista flew out of the country to his loot of some U.S. $700,000,000 which he had salted away in foreign banks.

Only a few shots had been fired, but he knew that he was already defeated. It was not so much the revolutionaries who had won as the dictator who had lost.

Batista's army surrendered, and suddenly Castro and his little band were the sole rulers of the sugar island. " I'll never forget his first speech," the doctor said. " He had a dove perched on his shoulder and he promised to make Cuba into a paradise for everyone. People went wild. How he was going to do it he did not say, beyond vague promises of reform. I don't think he really had a concrete programme. He solemnly promised never to nationalize industry and never to suppress even one civil right. And we believed him—he had the whole people in the hollow of his hand."

At first the revolutionaries concentrated their efforts on doing away with the worst of the evils of the dictatorship. Castro appointed a government of leading liberals, but kept the real power himself. He did away with corruption, reduced rents by fifty per cent, and reformed the tax system.

Many revolutionaries maintain that big business worked against Castro from the very start, but the doctor disagreed. He told us that a few weeks after the changeover, the leaders of industry decided to pay a year's tax in advance, thus putting U.S. $3,000,000 into the empty coffers which Batista had left behind. This enabled Castro to start action at once against Cuba's perennial problem : unemployment. Large-scale public works were started and, with the return of stability, the economy quickly took an upward turn.

Why did Castro not continue in this track? Some maintain it was because the United States pushed Castro into the arms of the Soviet Union. They thought that the seeds of discord were already sown on Castro's first visit to the United States shortly after his victory. He expected a hero's welcome and hoped for big loans—on his own conditions.

Only Vice-President Nixon came to meet him at the airport—and without a fanfare. The Press were generally unfavourable towards Castro because his régime had conducted mass executions of Batista's killers. There were no offers of loans, but a meeting with a group of congressmen was arranged for him. They patted him condescendingly on the back and let him understand that if he expected help from Uncle Sam he had to be a good boy and not tamper with American investments in Cuba . . .

Very sensible advice, if they had been dealing with one

of the usual Latin-American dictators, but it probably infuriated the sensitive and egocentric young idealist. Castro returned to Cuba at once, and from that day his attacks against the United States became increasingly more bitter. Soon afterwards the economic war broke out between the two countries, and the American-backed invasion last summer was merely the last of many American blunders.

" No one can deny that the North Americans acted stupidly and clumsily," the doctor continued thoughtfully. " But that does not explain why Castro is turning Cuba into a Communist state, with a muzzled press, no freedom of speech, vigilance committees and all the rest of it. He claims now that he has been a Communist for years, but I just don't believe it. I think he is introducing Communism because he has discovered that it is the only way he can stay in power."

He explained that the majority of the men who came down from the mountains with Castro had joined him only because they wanted to get rid of Batista. They were revolutionaries—not social reformers. When the victory had been won they asked their leader why he did not hold elections and hand over power to a civilian administration. That was what he had promised to do all along and then they could go home.

" You must remember that Castro's power at that time rested entirely on the revolutionary army," the doctor said. " He had either to follow the advice of his soldiers or seek support elsewhere. He chose the latter course.

" One can't help wondering why he refused to hold elections, for at the moment he would have won with a tremendous majority. I think it may be because he didn't feel like sharing the limelight with other politicians. Besides, he has always hated criticism, and he certainly could not have avoided that if he had thrown open the political arena.

"Almost without people noticing it he managed to change horses in midstream. He began by stripping many of his bearded veterans of their power. But whom was he to appoint in their places? His own party was already in dissolution and anyway, its members were mainly people who were against dictatorship in any form. He had practically no choice but to appoint Communists to the empty posts. They were able and disciplined and didn't care a hang about free elections. And they had a programme."

Every time one of Castro's former supporters criticized his policy, he rushed to the microphone and accused them of treachery. They were not given a chance to defend themselves. Before long, two-thirds of the members of the liberal government were in prison or in exile. A few of his former officers who openly accused him of introducing Communism were also given long prison terms. The revolutionary army was replaced by the youngsters of the people's militia, whose zeal was whipped up with Communist propaganda.

Although Communism is not working very well in Cuba, the doctor thought it quite possible that it would spread to other parts of the Western hemisphere. "I'm afraid it has a mission in some of the Latin-American countries," he said. "On the surface we are democracies, but our society really rests on a structure of feudalism which we have inherited from the Spanish occupation. That has to be changed before there can be any real progress. It looks as if the Communists are the only ones who are willing to tackle the job—and their price is freedom."

For some moments we stared straight ahead in gloomy silence. "It comforts me a little to think that at least it will be done by Latin-American Communists," the doctor then added, glancing towards the other table. "How heavy and depressing those people look—surely our own Communists will never become like them!"

My thoughts went back to a man I had once seen walking across a busy street in Mexico City with a ten-peso note in his hand. As he passed a policeman he gave him the money, which was the fine you had to pay for jay-walking. No one was going to tell him where he could go and where he couldn't . . .

"Yes, I think you are right," I said. "The Latin-Americans are quite different."

He nodded hopefully and we emptied our glasses.

"I think we might as well go home," I added, beckoning the waiter. "It looks as if Fidel won't be coming tonight, anyway."

CHAPTER SIX

THE WEED OF WISDOM

SEEN FROM A distance Kingston is one of the most beautiful cities in the West Indies. It lies on the south coast of Jamaica between the blue sea and a majestic chain of purple mountains. Most of the houses are quite low, and when the sun shines on them a strange, unearthly light shimmers above the roofs.

But when Chi-yun and I drove in from the airfield, which lies on an isthmus in the harbour, the town seemed to undergo a change in front of our very eyes. The motor road turned into a dirty street with an open sewer running on either side of it, and the mountains became hidden behind depressing, barrack-like houses, to which not even age and decay have managed to give a patina. The fascinating glimmer turned out to be merely reflection of sunlight from rusty corrugated iron roofs.

The car moved at a snail's pace in the steamy heat. Somewhere ahead there was a traffic jam, and no wonder, for the streets looked as if they had not been widened since the days of Queen Victoria. On the sidewalk endless rows of negroes moved by, perspiring in shabby European clothes. Wistfully we thought of the colourful garments of the negroes in Africa. They would certainly have brightened this ugly city!

Suddenly we saw a strange figure: an erect, half-naked

negro whose uncombed hair and beard seemed to be made up into many tiny plaits. In his right hand he held a staff which he raised threateningly as he stepped out on the road. The cars stopped, and with long, dignified steps he strode across.

Who on earth was that? I asked our black driver. A Ras Tafari, he replied—that was a religious sect which had members throughout Jamaica. They never cut their hair, they smoked marijuana—here it was called *ganja*—and their greatest desire was to return to Africa. The driver could not tell me the meaning of the word Ras Tafari, and when I asked him how I could get in touch with some members of the sect, his eyes widened. I had better keep away from the Ras Tafaris, he said. When they smoked they could be dangerous. They had killed several people, and they did not like the whites. He finally told me that there was a large group of them living in the harbour area not far from the power plant. Early the next morning, before the heat became too oppressive, I set out for their camp. To get there I had to cross a smoking garbage dump which separated it from the road.

The first glimpse of it made me think of Robert Jacobsen, the artist who makes his abstract sculptures out of scrap iron. The huts were lying close to the water; there must have been a couple of hundred of them and they were made chiefly out of flattened petrol tins and the remnants of motor cars. They looked as if the first gust of wind would blow them over, but they must have been stronger than I thought, or they would hardly have survived the hurricane which had struck Jamaica a few weeks previously.

The only people about were a couple of long-haired, half-naked boys playing " driving " in the rusty skeleton of a Chevrolet. At the sight of me they stiffened, then dashed away in between the huts. A moment later they returned with three bearded young negroes whose curly locks reached down to their shoulders.

My anxiety as to how they would receive me quickly disappeared, for they held out their arms and repeated the same word in a singsong voice: "*Love, love, love.*" But when I tried to take one of the outstretched hands it was immediately withdrawn. Who was I and what was I doing here? they demanded angrily, forming a circle around me. It seemed that the sweet word of love had only been a formal greeting.

My explanation that I was a journalist and wanted to learn something about their religion seemed to put them in a more friendly mood. They quickly exchanged a few sentences—at first I thought they were speaking a strange language, but it turned out to be English, only pronounced in a way that was incomprehensible to me. One of them made a sign for me to follow them, and with the two boys at our heels we walked down a dirty alley between the wretched dwellings.

Close to the water we stopped in front of a hut surrounded by a man-high rickety fence. The tallest one of the three pointed to a home-made sign above the entrance. *Ras Tafari Blood and Thunder Group* it said in clumsy lettering. *We want to go home to Africa—not as a favour, but as our right.*

This was their meeting place, they said, opening the gate which was hinged with two worn leather soles. The entrance to the hut was so low that we had to bow our heads to enter, and when I straightened up again my head bumped against the ceiling.

Slowly my eyes grew accustomed to the semi-darkness. The floor was of stamped earth and there was no furniture beyond some low, crude benches. In a corner were a couple of home-made musical instruments which looked somewhat like mandolins. Over the door hung a picture of a bearded man in colourful clothes and wearing a golden crown on his head. On the opposite wall was a newspaper clipping with a picture of Fidel Castro.

The tallest one of the three made a sign for me to sit down. He was a slim, well-built fellow with strong, almost aristocratic features—a black Roman. As soon as I had seated myself they began cross-examining me. How long had I been in Jamaica? What did I know about the Ras Tafaris? Was it simply by chance that I had come to their camp?

My replies seemed to satisfy them. They were willing to tell me about their faith, the tallest one said as he rose and pointed at the picture above the door. Solemnly he added: " This is our God—the King of Kings, the all-conquering Lion of Judah!"

" Ras Tafari!" they shouted in a chorus, stamping their feet. I was about to ask them who this Ras Tafari was when the tall negro raised his hand. They had not eaten since the previous day and had to have money for fruit and *ganja*. If they did not smoke they would not be able to communicate with their god, and *ganja* was not good on an empty stomach.

I took out three shillings. The tall negro smiled contemptuously. Nothing less than ten would do, he said. When I had given him the note he handed it without a word of thanks to one of the boys. He ran out to return some minutes later with a couple of green coconuts, a bunch of bananas and a small parcel which he produced from a fold of his ragged shirt. They ate ravenously and gulped down the coconut milk. Then they opened the little package, which contained some dark strips that looked like crude tobacco. They cut these into small pieces and stuffed it into a short clay pipe.

" Do you have any matches?" one of them said to me in Swedish. " Thank you very much," he added in the same language when I handed him a box. I asked in surprise where he had learned Swedish. What he had done before was not of any importance now, he replied with a wave of his hand. Ras Tafaris had no past—to them life did not really begin until the moment they joined the Movement. I suppose he had once worked on a Swedish ship.

He lit the pipe, inhaled deeply, and passed it on. Nearly a minute passed before he exhaled the smoke. It was seven years since I had smoked marijuana in Mexico in order to write about it, but the pungent smell at once brought back the memory. When the pipe reached me I felt very much like taking a puff, but refused after a moment of hesitation. There was work to be done.

The two boys also smoked, and their practised way of doing it showed that it was not the first time. Three times the pipe was refilled and passed around. It was a huge dose, even considering how many they were, but though I watched them closely I could not notice any change in them except that they breathed a little faster than before.

The smaller boy cannot have been more than six years old. When he took the pipe for the third time I put my hand on his shoulder to suggest that he had had enough. He leaped away from me.

" Don't touch me!" he hissed.

The three grown-ups leaned back on the benches and looked at the ceiling. For the next couple of hours they talked incessantly, either one at a time, or simultaneously. Though I scribbled away I had trouble in getting it all down in my notebook.

The Jews called themselves God's chosen people, they said,

but they had no right to do so, for God was really black. This was clearly stated in the original Bible, which had been re-written and falsified by a white man : King James I of England. In fact the promised land lay in Africa, and the Ras Tafaris were God's chosen people . . .

Again they jumped up and stamped their feet. " Ras Tafari, the King of Kings, the all-conquering Lion of Judah!" they shouted, bowing before the picture over the door. They were streaming with perspiration and their bodies gave off a strong rancid odour. They explained that the man in the picture was Ras Tafari, which was the name of the Emperor of Ethiopia before he was crowned. He was the re-incarnation of God and the father of the bearded brothers. Once in the remote past they had sinned against him however, and as punishment he had sent them into exile. As slaves they had been shipped across the sea to the new world . . .

One of them let out a yell and hid his face in his hands. " I feel it !" he shouted. " The whip is biting my back !"

Though I smiled only fleetingly it did not escape the tall negro. He leaned closer to me and stared into my eyes. It seemed to me that his pupils were twice as large as before.

" You think we can't remember our former lives," he said. " But those who smoke the weed of wisdom know everything that is, always has been, and always will be. The past is in us and the future is in us too—you understand ?"

I nodded. From my own experience with marijuana I clearly remembered this feeling of immortality. Somehow they must have sensed that I understood them, for the three black faces were softened by smiles. I might, despite my colour, be converted and join their brotherhood, one of them said eagerly. And was I sure that I did not have an African fore-father way back? I mostly likely did, they agreed, for otherwise how could I have such a great understanding of the truth?

The next moment I spoiled it by asking them when their religion had been founded. They clutched their heads and asked angrily how something could have been founded when it had always been? I quickly re-phrased it to, " When was it discovered that Ras Tafari was the re-incarnation of God?"

In the early part of the First Great War, they replied. Kaiser Wilhelm of Germany had come riding to Africa at the head of a great army which everyone had thought invincible. On a beach he had seen the Crown Prince of Ethiopia, Ras Tafari, who was kneeling in prayer. A white light from heaven had fallen upon him, and at once Kaiser Wilhelm had realized that here he had found his superior. He threw himself into the dust before Ras Tafari and then went away with his army.

But the time had not been ripe for the final victory of Ras Tafari. His children had had to undergo many trials, and were still doing so. At the moment, Babylon was on top . . .

Babylon? Yes—they also called it " the four beasts." By this they meant England, the United States, France and Russia. In their eyes there was only a slight difference between them, because they were all equally materialistic. " They worship the same golden calf," was how they expressed it.

Ras Tafari had selected Russia as the instrument with which to destroy the colonial powers. When this had been brought about, the Russians would not remain on the pinnacle of victory, however, for their barren materialism carried the seeds of its own destruction.

But long before the fall of " the four beasts," the Ras Tafari brethren would be back in Africa. Their Emperor would send a great ship for them—it was because they wanted to be ready for this that they were living so close to the sea. One of them thought it more likely that he would send an airship, a great chariot of fire, but that would make no difference, because the airfield was also near by.

" Ras Tafari, the King of Kings, the all-conquering Lion of Judah!" they shouted with shining eyes. " Take us away from here—home to your kingdom which flows with milk and honey!"

To them Jamaica was hell, for here they were hated and persecuted by those in power, even though they harmed no one. They lived peacefully in their camps, without women— members of the weaker sex did not participate in their religious ceremonies. They did not beg and eschewed alcohol, salt and pork.

Despite this, people would not give them work and many Ras Tafari brethren were in prison. Again and again the police had torn their huts down because they were built on public land, " even the garbage dumps are thought to be too good for us!" they said bitterly. When they were arrested the police often forcibly cut off their long hair and beards. The accusations against them are always the same—that they smoked *ganja*—but this was an essential part of their religious worship. Nothing, neither bullets nor the gallows, could stop them from doing so.

The tall negro rose. " We do not fear prison, because freedom lives inside us," he shouted. " But our patience will soon be at an end. If the persecution goes on we will take revenge —and I tell you, we have the power to do so!"

He shook his fist in the direction of the city. " Woe unto thee, Babylon—the moon will be bathed in blood and you will lie in darkness!"

" Ras Tafari!" they shouted again. I now pointed at the

74

clipping of Fidel Castro and told them that I had just been to Cuba. Eagerly they asked me how black people were treated over there. " The same as the whites," I replied. They smiled and nodded to each other.

" He is one of us," the tall one said. " He is bearded, too!"

I began to describe the revolutionary régime's rural reforms, but that did not seem to interest them. They thought of Castro merely as an instrument in a global racial struggle. If they had to use force in securing what they considered their rights they counted on support from him. They were willing to accept help from anybody.

Would it be all right for me to take some pictures of them? They could not give me permission, they replied, but if I would return in the afternoon when they were going to have a meeting I could ask one of the elder brethren.

The Swedish-speaking negro accompanied me to the road. Many eyes followed us from the other huts and several people asked who I was. " A friend," he replied. " When you are with a Ras Tafari brother you have nothing to fear from the poor," he added.

After lunch I went to the central police station to get some information about the Ras Tafaris. I was shown in to a sergeant, a friendly mulatto who had a thick dossier before him. It was not known exactly when the movement had started, he said, slowly turning over the pages. One of the first " prophets " had been a lay preacher who had had a rather large following in Kingston in the twenties. He had talked of Africa as the Promised Land, but neither he nor his followers had worn beards or long hair. Finally he had attempted to fly back to Africa from a tall building and had ended in a mental institution with a broken leg.

During the Italian attack on Ethiopia, which had caused

great indignation among the negroes in Jamaica, a new prophet had arisen, a huge negro by the name of Howell. He had sold pictures of the Emperor of Ethiopia for a shilling each and guaranteed that they could also be used as tickets for going back to Africa. Before he was arrested for fraud and sentenced to two years' imprisonment he had sold some five thousand of them.

When he was released he went to an uninhabited place with a couple of thousand of his followers, who were mostly extremely poor people. They built a mansion for him where he lorded it over a harem of thirteen women, while they themselves lived in wretched huts. It was around this time that the Ras Tafari movement got its name and the members began to grow long hair and beards, probably inspired by the pictures of Haile Selassie. The believers kept cattle and raised grain and vegetables, but *ganja* was their main source of income. Up until then this narcotic had not been widely used, but during the following years its popularity increased steadily, despite severe punishment meted out to those caught growing, selling or smoking it.

When a *ganja* case came up, the source of supply was almost invariably traced to Howell's camp, and in 1947 a large force of policemen was sent there to arrest him. The bearded ones resisted and only after a fierce struggle did the law enforcers succeed in apprehending the " prophet," who was declared insane and sent to the same mental institution as his predecessor.

After the dissolution of the colony the ragged, bearded men became a common sight all over the island. What did they live on? The sergeant shrugged. Only a few had regular work. The rest sold *ganja* or earned a little money by collecting rags, bottles and old iron at the garbage dumps.

The Weed of Wisdom

How many Ras Tafaris were there? Some said a couple of thousand, others said at least twenty thousand, but everyone agreed that the number was increasing. Quite a few common criminals pretended to be Ras Tafaris. This was an excellent disguise and they could count on help from the poor, who were generally friendly disposed towards the brethren.

Three years ago it had been rumoured among the Ras Tafaris that soon the Emperor's ship was coming to collect them. Some three thousand of the bearded ones from all over the island had gathered in Kingston to hold themselves in readiness for the departure. Every night for a week they sat up and waited around bonfires of old automobile tyres. It was rumoured that they had sacrificed one or two children by throwing them into the flames, probably to placate the higher powers so that the ship would come, but the police had no proof. So many orphans were running about in Kingston, and those who might know about it preferred not to talk.

Finally the police had to put out the fires for fear they would spread. In their disappointment that the ship had not come the Ras Tafaris set upon the police and several people were severely wounded.

Shortly afterwards the authorities sent a delegation to Ethiopia to ask the Emperor if he would accept emigrants from Jamaica. Haile Selassie replied that his country could only use skilled workers, and asked the delegates to tell the Ras Tafaris that he was no living god. This the bearded ones stubbornly refused to believe—they were convinced that the delegation was fooling them.

Not many think it likely that the Ras Tafaris will revolt or try to seize power, but some were afraid that they might be made use of by others who had such plans. Thus, a couple of years ago a young Jamaican returned from a visit to the

77

United States accompanied by two American negroes. The trio had some vague plan of starting a Castro-style rebellion to liberate the island from the whites. The Ras Tafari movement must have seemed suitable for this purpose, for they only sought recruits among the bearded ones and began to train about fifty of them in a camp in the hills.

Before long the police heard of strange happenings in the camp, and when troops were sent there they were met by bullets. The three leaders escaped, but were caught some days later. During the ensuing court case it was revealed that they had accused two Ras Tafaris of treason and had " executed " them. The three young negroes were hanged for this crime.

Before I left we talked of the possibility that Communist agents might capitalize on the ignorance of the Ras Tafaris. This could easily happen, for the bearded ones represent the dissatisfied elements in a society which has an ideal setting for a class struggle, since the economic division of the population coincides with the racial one.

Jamaica, which is about one-fifth the size of Denmark, is crowded with close to two million inhabitants. The Europeans, who form slightly over one per cent, are on the whole quite wealthy—and thus naturally fall into the category of white capitalists. The middle class is, broadly speaking, made up of twenty per cent of the population and are mostly mulattos —the brown bourgeoisie. The remaining eighty per cent are negroes—the black proletariat . . .

A little later in the afternoon I returned to the meeting place of the Ras Tafaris. " Love, love, love," I heard from all sides as I entered the hut. The benches were now occupied by about twenty ragged men with long hair and beards. I could smell that they had just been smoking *ganja*.

The Weed of Wisdom

A middle-aged negro with bright intelligent eyes asked me to sit down. I think he was their leader, for he wanted to know exactly what the three others had told me during the morning. Every word I had written in my notebook had to be read aloud to him. He listened with half-closed eyes, breaking in every now and again to make a correction or to add something.

When I was nearly through, a young, almost beardless Ras Tafari came into the hut. At the sight of me he began to talk excitedly. He had seen me at the police station! Everybody began to shout, but the middle-aged negro raised his hand for silence. In the stillness that followed one could hear the rumbling of the nearby power-plant.

" What were you doing at the police station?" he asked. I explained that as a journalist I had to get information from many different sources, also from the authorities. What had they told me at the police station? A lot of things—it took up more than two pages in my notebook.

" Read it to us!" he snapped. They listened avidly, and several burst out laughing when I reached the place where it said that there were between two thousand and twenty thousand Ras Tafaris.

" We are many, many more," the middle-aged negro said. " Don't think that all of us have long hair and beards. And for every one of us there are ten who side with us. All the poor consider us their leaders."

I read on, but was interrupted again, this time by a shout from a guard who had been posted outside. Three policemen were approaching the camp!

The men jumped up and produced small hoards of *ganja* from their manes or beards or from their clothes. Quickly they wrapped it in a newspaper which they handed to a boy

79

who disappeared with it. Then they turned to me. Their accusing glances said more clearly than words that they thought I was a police agent. An informer!

It suddenly occurred to me that the situation could be dangerous, but just then the voice outside shouted that it was a false alarm, the policemen had driven on. I think I heaved a deeper sigh of relief than anybody else in the hut. When I had finished reading my notes I was told that it was all right for me to photograph them and we went outside. Someone had brought along a green, red and yellow flag which they insisted on holding in the pictures.

" This is the Ethiopian flag," the middle-aged man explained, stroking it gently. " We don't recognize any other."

They stood with their heads proudly raised in the last rays of the afternoon sun, a small group of poor, dirty men. Behind them, through the dust from the garbage dump, I could make out the purple mountains whose slopes were divided into thousands of tiny lots. It is there that one finds the roots of the Ras Tafari movement, I thought.

The population of the mountainous little island doubles every fifty years or so, but there is no more land which can be brought under cultivation, nor is there any appreciable industry which can give employment to the many idle hands. In their fruitless groping for a solution, the poorest of the negroes have turned to their lost paradise, Africa. There they hope, perhaps subconsciously, to find the soul which the black man lost when he was torn away from his own culture. But Africa does not want them back . . .

Before I left I gave them two pounds sterling. They did not thank me, and in a way I was glad. At that moment I felt that a great deal more than alms was necessary to pay the debt that I owed them as a European.

. From our visit to the Caribs on the island of Dominica. This young girl removed the top with her teeth when I offered her a bottle.

10. Visiting the Redlegs in Barbados. The bright glare disclosed running sores on all legs and arms. It is Mrs. Gibson behind the children.

. Pundit Sadhu was formerly a poor agricultural labourer. Since he made his way as spiritual adviser and faith-healer he has become a rich man.

12. The soil of many of the Caribbean islands is fertile, but the only tool known by the uneducated farmers is a hoe. The standard of living is very poor – in Haiti where this photo was taken the average annual income is less than twenty pounds.

CHAPTER SEVEN

THE GILDED AFRICAN

ON OUR JOURNEYS to Africa my wife and I have met many Europeans who are convinced that the negroes are our inferiors in every respect.

" The blacks are all right as long as you keep an eye on them," they say, " but they are incapable of doing anything independently. They just don't know how to organize."

I wish some of those whites had accompanied us on our trip to Haiti. Then they would hardly be so sure any more, for in this poverty-stricken republic one still finds the remnants of a great negro civilization. Giant fortresses and lovely castles were built by ex-slaves who also founded one of the best-organized states of their day.

Haiti's period of greatness coincides approximately with the French revolution. The country was then inhabited by about thirty thousand whites, four hundred thousand negro slaves and fifty thousand mulattos who lived in the twilight between the two groups. True, they were free, but they could only attain the lowest positions and were not even permitted to dress like the whites. This was of course a thorn in their flesh, as many of them were gifted people. For instance, Alexander Dumas, who was a mulatto, was of Haitian descent.

An excellent irrigation system made the white planters

more or less independent of the rainfall. Seven hundred trading ships were busy sailing the riches of Haiti—sugar—to the mother country. They returned laden with European luxuries which even the members of the French court could hardly afford to buy.

When the news of the revolution reached Haiti the whites tried at first to keep it secret from the rest of the population. They realized that if the golden promises of the revolution were fulfilled, it would spell the doom of a colonial system which was based on exploitation and racial segregation. More than a century and a half were to pass before we Europeans began to put into practice the great ideals of liberty, equality and fraternity on other continents.

It soon came to the ears of the mulattos that France had a new government with liberal ideas. They managed to send representatives to Paris, where they requested more rights for their group. This was granted, but the whites in Haiti refused to carry out the orders of the National Convention. Two young mulattos who publicly protested against this were seized and executed—an act which the whites were soon to regret.

When the National Convention in France finally got round to sending representatives to Haiti, they had several royalist planters executed in front of a great throng. According to an eye-witness account from those days, the blacks and the mulattos at first thought that the guillotine was a plaything. When they saw the heads roll they screamed in terror, then stormed forward and tore it apart.

Perhaps the slaves understood that the whites were now divided among themselves, for they rebelled shortly afterwards. If the mulattos had sided with the whites or remained neutral, the French could probably have held their own. But the half-breeds, knowing from bitter experience that the whites would not do anything for them, joined in with the negroes, whom they really despised.

The revolt quickly spread over the whole island. In a few days, between three and four thousand Frenchmen lost their lives, and in some places people were literally wading in blood. "It looked as if the blacks wore crimson gloves and stockings," one of the survivors later wrote. The smoke and the reflection of the fires from the burning plantation buildings could be seen hundreds of miles away in the Bahamas, where people thought that there had been a volcanic eruption.

When the rebellion was a few months old the first of Haiti's two great leaders, Toussaint, stepped into the limelight. Most people called him *l'Ouverture* (The Gap), probably because several of his front teeth were missing. He was a small, middle-aged negro with a monkey-like face.

During the rebellion he had hidden his white master from the vindictive slaves. He was a great admirer of French culture and the French revolution and wanted to bind Haiti even closer to the mother country—but as an equal.

Toussaint's oratorical gifts soon won him a following among the blacks. His first great achievement was to turn a band of ragged slaves into a well-disciplined army. With its aid, he managed in a surprisingly short time to create order out of the chaos that had followed in the wake of the rebellion. To get the sugar production going again he sent his troops to work on the plantations. He appointed many mulattos to leading positions and did everything in his power to create confidence between black and brown. That the attempt failed was Haiti's tragedy.

The situation was extremely complicated, for officially the island was still ruled by a French Governor, apart from the eastern section which was under Spain and was later to become the Dominican Republic. The French made several attempts to reassert their power in the colony, but their forces were no match for Toussaint's army, which eventually counted close to twenty thousand.

When the British landed a large force in Haiti, Toussaint immediately rushed to the aid of the Governor, who showed his appreciation by making the negro leader his second-in-command. After this there was rapid improvement in the relationship between the revolutionary government in France and the former colony. In 1801 Haiti was granted a constitution, which Toussaint wisely had drawn up by seven whites and three mulattos.

But now the shadow of Napoleon fell on Haiti. He was jealous of " the gilded African," as he contemptuously called Toussaint, and in 1802 sent a great fleet with twenty-five thousand veterans to Haiti. The French quickly conquered the larger towns, but the blacks continued resisting in the mountains. After some months the leader of the invasion force invited Toussaint to the conference table, promising him good terms and safe conduct.

As soon as Toussaint came on board the French warship in which the negotiations were to take place, it set sail for Europe. This was done on the explicit orders of Napoleon, but Toussaint refused to believe that the French First Consul, of whom he was a great admirer, knew of the treachery. Long after he had been imprisoned in a fortress in the Jura mountains, he continued to appeal to Napoleon in letters written in clumsy French. Napoleon did not bother to read them, but many years later, when he was at St. Helena, he said that his treatment of Toussaint was one of the few things he regretted in his life. By then the little negro had long since died of tuberculosis.

The Gilded African

At first the loss of their leader had a paralyzing effect on the blacks, but when the French attempted to re-introduce slavery, the whole population rose in fury against the whites. They found an unexpected ally in yellow fever, which mowed down the European soldiers but curiously enough hardly affected the negroes or the mulattos. In 1803 the last French troops sailed away and Haiti declared its independence as the first negro republic in the world.

With Toussaint no longer there to mediate, the smouldering enmity between brown and black turned into a blaze. During the ensuing civil war, which ended with the temporary partition of the country, one of Toussaint's generals seized power and had himself crowned as Emperor. He became so hated, however, that his own soldiers murdered him two years later. Now came the turn of the second of Haiti's great sons, Christophe.

White men who visited him when he was at the height of his career agreed that he possessed great natural dignity. Perhaps this was because Christophe had never known the indignities of slavery. This nearly seven-foot tall negro, whose skin was the colour of ebony, was the son of a freed slave from one of the British West Indian islands. Not much is known about his youth except that he fought as a volunteer in the American revolutionary war—on the side of the British. Later on he showed his predilection for everything English by taking Henry as his first name—not the French Henri.

When the Haitian negroes rebelled he was a waiter at a hotel in a large port city. He joined Toussaint and quickly rose to become a general, partly because of his exceptional organizing ability and partly because there were so few negroes who could read and write. After the fall of the tyrannical Emperor he ruled for four years as President and then had himself crowned King. During the thirteen years of his rule, greater progress was made than during the whole of the following century.

Today Christophe is often described as a heartless dictator. He was indeed both ruthless and self-willed, but he understood his people and knew that only by leading them to greatness could he cure them of the inferiority complex of the slave. His ambition was to make Haiti the equal of the white nations.

One of his first acts as King was to create a black aristocracy of eight dukes, twenty-two counts and thirty-seven barons. He then gave the country a new set of laws, and according to evil tongues, Paragraph One in *Code Henry* prescribed that no one was to appear at court except in full uniform and that no two uniforms were to be alike.

This is of course an exaggeration, but there were exact regulations as to how each rank was to dress. The costumes and gowns were made of the finest brocades and silks, and were decorated with ostrich feathers and epaulettes of pure gold. Thus Christophe, who personally dressed rather plainly, killed two birds with one stone. He gave the negroes the splendour and magnificence which they craved and simultaneously struck a blow at the laziness which was a natural consequence of slavery. The uniforms and gowns were exceedingly costly, and to be able to pay for them the members of the new *élite* were forced to make as much as possible out of the estates which went along with the fine titles.

" Thus, vanity is here the motive power," wrote an Englishman who visited Haiti at that time.

Great care was taken that the noblemen did not abuse the people under them. A ten-hour working day was established by law, and no one was to labour from Saturday noon until Monday morning.

The nobility also had to look after the old and weak. If any tried to shirk his responsibility, the news would soon reach the ear of Christophe, who gave audience to the common people once a week. Several members of the *élite* were condemned to work side by side with the people on their own estates until they had learned *noblesse oblige*.

With the new noblemen at the helm, the sugar production increased many-fold, but Christophe seems to have realized the danger of being dependent on a single crop. He introduced an economic reform programme surprisingly like the one Fidel Castro is now trying to carry out in Cuba. The plantations were ordered to grow new crops, mainly coffee, cocoa and cotton. With the aid of foreign experts, new industries were started to prevent the unemployment in the " dead " season. Thus an entire cotton spinnery was imported from Manchester.

And, like the Cuban revolutionaries, Christophe started an impressive educational campaign. Several foreign teachers were employed at the numerous new schools built during his rule. In those days there was compulsory education, and it is said that when Christophe died the majority of the Haitians could read and write. Today, more than ninety per cent of them are illiterate.

The inexhaustible Christophe also started a state printing house, an art academy and he built a fleet. He created provincial courts under a Supreme Court and divided the government into ministries. One wonders how he found the means for all this, for when he came to power the treasury was empty and there was practically no money in circulation, the people having reverted to bartering.

Christophe produced hard cash in an unorthodox, but highly effective way. First he ordered all calabashes—in Haiti they are called *gourds*—to be handed over to the government. This did not create opposition, for the calabashes were mostly used for the collection of coffee berries and the coffee had just been harvested.

Christophe's officials collected over a quarter of a million calabashes which he had stamped as twenty *sous* each. When the next coffee harvest was ripe and the farmers began to feel the need of containers, Christophe announced that he would return the calabashes against the equivalent of twenty *sous* worth of coffee berries for each one. The negroes found this reasonable enough, calabashes now being so scarce, and the gold which Christophe earned by selling the coffee abroad he had struck into coins.

Today the Haitians use mostly U.S. dollars, but they still speak of twenty cents as *un gourde.*

Though Christophe himself does not seem to have been religious, he realized the necessity of his people having a faith. Under him *voodoo,* a primitive religion based on conjuring up the ancient African spirits, was prohibited. It had been a great comfort to the negroes during the days of slavery, but Christophe felt that in the long run it would keep the people in ignorance and backwardness.

Catholicism was made the state religion and men and women were prohibited from living together without the blessings of the church. This caused great opposition. The former white masters, to whom the negro women had been a kind of breeding animal, had prohibited the slaves from marrying, so the negroes had come to prefer " free " love. Later, after the death of the King, this was one of the first laws to be ignored.

Christophe loved to build new and ever grander houses, many of which are standing to this day. One of the first ones was a palace he built for himself and his Queen. *Sans Souci,* he called it, and judging by the ruins, it was even more beautiful than Frederick the Great's famous summer palace of the same name in Potsdam.

An old painting of Christophe and his Court shows the main hall at *Sans Souci* brightly illuminated with sparkling chandeliers. In the centre of the picture stands the King, a black giant wearing a plain blue jacket and tight white trousers. He stretches one arm towards his wife, a proud and beautiful negress not quite as dark as her husband. Their two daughters, the Princesses Athenaire and Amethyst, look as if they are just about to curtsy to the Court Doctor, a skinny Scotsman. In the background, along walls panelled in velvet, stand the black noblemen and their ladies in splendid attire.

Besides *Sans Souci* Christophe built six other palaces and several fortresses. By far the greatest of these is " The Citadel," which lies on a mountain top more than half a mile above sea level. When Chi-yun and I reached there after a long ride on horseback, we felt as if we were returning to the Middle Ages. The ninety-foot-tall main wall, of which one angle is shaped like the prow of a ship, seemed to jut out of the very cliffs. High above it the clouds sailed serenely by.

A long, dark staircase led to cold halls and draughty half-open corridors where gigantic rusty cannon stood with their muzzles pointing out over the green valley which the fortress used to control; and when we shone our flashlight down the cellars we could see great heaps of cannon balls. How Christophe managed to get the guns up here is a puzzle, for some of them weigh several tons. Some years ago, the Haitian government decided to sell them as scrap iron, but had to give up the idea as it proved too difficult to transport them down over the narrow mountain paths.

The fortress, which could house ten thousand soldiers and enough supplies for several years, must have demanded a greater effort than all of Christophe's other construction works put together. The fear which Napoleon inspired in the Haitian leaders was great. He had attempted once to reconquer the lost colony, and who knew when he might try to do so again? Christophe realized that his army could not prevent the European soldiers from over-running the lowlands, and he had probably planned to continue the struggle from the impregnable fortress if the French returned.

Many believe that it was the Citadel which finally broke Christophe, and undoubtedly it contributed to his downfall. The new nation simply could not support it. Another contributory factor was that the people were tired of his iron discipline and of the ceaseless wars with the mulattos who held part of the country.

On a Sunday afternoon in 1820 it was rumoured that the King had suffered a stroke. At once a large crowd of his opponents gathered outside *Sans Souci,* hopefully awaiting the news of his death. Christophe must have been able to hear their voices as he lay paralyzed in his bedroom. The Scottish doctor tried many remedies, but finally had to admit defeat. Now a black medicine man was sent for, and for hours he massaged the King with red pepper. It must have burned like fire.

Towards morning Christophe whispered that he felt life returning to his limbs. He ordered his guards to march to the front of the palace. Wearing his uniform and with a sabre dangling from his waist, he walked across the lawn towards his white charger, but collapsed a few steps from it. The crowd screamed in triumph. He waved aside those who rushed forward to support him and managed to walk back to his quarters unaided. A moment later a shot rang out. The King was dead.

With his death ended the greatness of Haiti. The mulattos conquered his kingdom and during the ensuing hundred years' war between black and brown, the irrigation system disintegrated, the harbours filled up with sand and erosion destroyed the once fertile land.

In 1915, after a three-year period during which one President had been poisoned, one blown to bits, one torn to pieces by a mob, and three forced to abdicate, the United States felt compelled to intervene. The following fifteen years under U.S. military government were the most peaceful in the history of the negro state, but when the Americans withdrew the quarrelling began again. Politics once again became a racial struggle, and in the end a small group of blacks succeeded in gaining power. They form a new upper-class which exploits the people mercilessly. Thousands of mulattos have had to go into exile.

Haiti, which is barely half the size of Denmark, is today one of the poorest countries in the world, with an average income of less than twenty pounds sterling a year. Six million ragged farmers scrape a bare existence from the exhausted soil. Every night the voodoo drums echo in the mountains. The American tourists listen spell-bound in their luxury hotels. They don't know what lies behind the weird ceremonies— that the people, as in the time of slavery, are seeking consolation and oblivion by conjuring up the spirits of Africa.

In Castro's Cuba, a few hundred miles away, a force of exiled Haitians are being trained in revolutionary tactics. Haiti—the proud land of Toussaint and Christophe, first to break the white man's chains—is to be liberated once more, but this time from its own black oppressors.

CHAPTER EIGHT

THE CRUISE OF THE "CHRISTINE"

ALL THAT WE knew about Puerto Rico, the next place we visited, we had read in a book by John Gunther. It almost stopped us from going there. We had already seen so much poverty on our journey, but judging by the famous American author it was nothing compared to what was in store for us.

"A blemish on Uncle Sam," he called the island, which has been under the Americans since they took it from Spain in 1898. It is about the size of the Danish isle of Zealand and has about two and a half million inhabitants. Gunther described the majority of them as living in sheds which would make the poorest hut in Calcutta look like a palace by comparison.

When we landed at Puerto Rico after an hour's flying from primitive Haiti, we felt as if we had put several centuries behind us. The airport was as modern as any in Europe. Along a broad highway and between rows of flashy American cars we drove to the capital, San Juan. Beautiful villas in the suburbs were followed by white apartment houses with open verandas and large windows. Where were the tumble-down corrugated iron shacks which had shocked John Gunther?

They have all disappeared, for since he wrote his book a miracle has taken place in Puerto Rico. Shortly after the last

World War, Uncle Sam decided to do something for his adopted Latin-American child. This may have been partly in the hope of slowing down the stream of Puerto Rican emigrants who were creating problems in New York.

The removal of the blemish demanded many remedies, among them local self-government, but most important was a law exempting Puerto Rican industry from American taxation. Until then the island had virtually existed on the sugar production, but now industrialists from the mainland began to build factories. The Puerto Ricans, who had a reputation for being lazy, proved be be excellent workers. They were used to going idle most of the year after the harvesting of the sugar cane, so to them steady work was like manna from heaven. They were satisfied with a fraction of what the American workers earned.

Quickly the word spread among U.S. businessmen that Puerto Rico now deserved its name : *Rich Harbour*. Factory chimneys rose everywhere on the island. With the growing competition for labour, wages rose until they are now the highest of any Latin-American country with the exception of Venezuela. Simultaneously the stream of emigrants to New York began to slow down, and lately some Puerto Ricans have even been going home to enjoy the new prosperity.

We would have liked to spend some days in the cosy old section of Puerto Rico, where one can still see the house that Cortez lived in before he set out to conquer the Aztec empire. This proved impossible, however, for I had decided to continue the journey by native schooner, and the day after our arrival I found an opportunity to ship out.

Chi-yun wanted very much to join me, but it was the stormy season and she is not a good sailor. She bought a ticket for a large passenger boat going to Trinidad, the southernmost of the Caribbean islands, where we agreed to meet when my cruise was over.

After waving goodbye to her I rushed down to the schooner called *Christine*. It would be leaving at three sharp, I had been told at the shipping office, and there were only a couple of minutes to go when I climbed on board, soaked with perspiration, for it was a hot, dead calm day.

I have seen many ugly ships in my time, but none that could compete with the *Christine*. It—to call it *she* would be an insult to the fair sex—was shaped like a bathtub and dirty grey where you could make out the original colour through the layers of dirt. Climbing over some rusty oil drums which were heaped on the deck, I came upon seven half-naked negroes who were playing cards in the shade of the wheelhouse.

I was going along as a passenger, I told them. Aha, they were sure glad to hear that, they replied, smiling broadly, and then went on playing. Perhaps they had not understood me, I thought, stepping over to the only one wearing a shirt. I had been told to give my ticket to the captain, I continued, handing it to him.

No people can laugh like the negroes, and now all seven started as if by command. Cackling and hooting, they slapped their thighs, their bodies bent double like folding knives.

"He thinks you're the captain!" they groaned, pointing at the shirt-clad negro, a tall fellow whose tiny curls looked like the wool on a new-born lamb. He made several attempts to say something, but could not get it out for laughing.

"I—I'm the cook," he finally managed to stutter. "That's the captain—we don't leave until he's sober."

He pointed at a mulatto lying on the floor of the wheelhouse. Even from where I stood I could smell the reek of rum. Carrying my suitcase in one hand I went to a little cabin amidships.

"Hello," someone said when I entered. On the floor sat two blond young men wearing nothing but their underpants. In drawling American they advised me to take my clothes off too, or they would become soiled immediately.

Looking around, I discovered that they were right. There was literally not a clean spot anywhere. The floor was hidden beneath a layer of filth mixed with the droppings of rats, and when I leaned against the door I got engine grease all over my elbow. I was amazed to see a brass plate stating that the *Christine* had been built in 1958. It seemed incredible that a ship could have become so dirty in only three years.

The tiny cabin contained neither table nor chair, and of the six bunks only the two bottom ones were in a usable condition, the rest lacked mattresses as well as bed-boards. The electrical generator had broken down and the toilet did not work, the two Americans informed me gloomily, so one had to do one's errands over the side.

Putting most of my clothes away in my suitcase, I sat down next to the two others. It would not be a comfortable journey, but I found comfort in the thought that the worse conditions one travels under, the more one gets to write about.

The two Americans were students going to an island called Antigua, a few hundred miles to the East, where they had obtained holiday jobs on the yacht of a rich man. When I heard that they came from Alabama I began telling them about my experiences there on a motoring trip some years back. Several times I had come close to being arrested because I spent so much time in the negro sections of the towns, and the negroes had been equally suspicious of me because I was white.

I found my account quite amusing until I discovered that the two boys were staring stiffly ahead of them. I must have hurt them in some way or other, I thought, and quickly added that this was many years ago, of course things had improved since then. Many whites must now realize that the racial barriers have to be removed . . .

Not in Alabama, they retorted—there people knew how to keep the coloured people in their place. But if that was the way they felt about it, why did they travel on this ship? I had thought that it was for the same reason I did—to get in contact with negroes.

No, sir! Their money had been stolen on a binge a few days back, so they were forced to go by this filthy nigger-boat.

I rose angrily and went out on deck. "You know how to play rummy, sir?" One of the negroes shouted, and when I nodded they enlarged their circle to make room for me. Though they did not play for stakes they went in for the game wholeheartedly. Every time someone picked up a card, he would look at it for several seconds, narrowed-eyed, scratching his neck. You could almost hear the creaking beneath the kinky hair. The winner would emit a scream of triumph and bang his cards on to the deck, one by one, while the others loudly bemoaned their poor luck.

My bewildered expression when they talked to each other caused them great amusement. One moment it sounded like French, the next like Spanish, and some words were completely strange to me. The cook explained that they were speaking *Papiemento,* a primitive language understood throughout the West Indies. It is composed of expressions from English, Dutch, Portuguese, Spanish, French and a couple of African dialects.

When we had played a few rounds the skipper began to

sober up, and around five o'clock we steamed out of the harbour, cooled by the breeze which we ourselves created. Behind us hung a tail of black smoke, and on land the sun was hiding her face behind green fields.

Just before darkness fell the cook called us over to a tiny galley where a primus had been hissing for some time. The crew ate with their fingers from a common pot, but we passengers were served our share in a bowl. Unfortunately there were no plates, the cook said, but he did have spoons for us.

We each began from one side and quickly worked our way towards the middle, for the sea air had made us hungry. It was a kind of stew made of fried rice, yams and bully beef. People say you can get used to anything, but I must admit that during the following days I came to appreciate this dish less and less; for it was the only thing we were served, apart from coffee and stale bread in the morning.

After dinner, when I made my way to the stern, the cook came and sat down next to me. He was afraid the food had not been very good he said, adding that he was not a cook by profession. He had gone to high school and was really a clerk, but it was nearly impossible to find a good job ashore. Throughout the islands, most of the people were out of work except during the sugar harvest. Wages, in any case, were so low that one could hardly exist on them.

Here he was paid thirty-five dollars a month (a West Indian dollar is worth about four shillings), not so bad considering that he got free board and lodging. The ship belonged to an Englishman who owned four other schooners. He made big money—he had a big house and a motor-car, and sent his sons to school in England—but he wouldn't spend a penny on repairing the ship.

D   97

How much did the others earn? The captain made fifty dollars a month, the engineer forty-five, the rest of the crew twenty-five. Sailors from my country probably made much more? Yes, I replied.

" Oh, well, but then they're white," he said, nodding to himself. White people always got the best jobs, that was the way it was. The brown ones, the mulattos, got the second-best. The whites and the browns had all the money and decided everything.

While the languid sea shone phosphorescently and bright, glowing sparks from the chimney flew towards the stars he taught me a little rhyme which I was later to hear again several times in the West Indies:

> *God made you, little nigger*
> *He made you in the night,*
> *He made you in a hurry*
> *And forgot to make you white . . .*

Suddenly we heard a furious shout from the wheel-house. The skipper had discovered that the sailor who was supposed to hoist the ship's lantern had forgotten to do so, so all this time we had been sailing without a light!

When we went amidships again the two Americans were standing outside the cabin, swearing. Where were they to sleep? The two usable bunks were full of snoring members of the crew. The cook explained that the *Christine* usually carried only plantation workers who slept on deck. When occasionally there were white passengers they would bring their own sleeping bags.

But he would try to fix things for us, he continued, shaking his sleeping comrades. When they woke he said a few words to them in Papiemento. Yawning, they got up and went out-side.

The Americans settled down on one of the still warm mat-tresses, I on the other. For a while I lay there and hated them in the darkness. What right did they have to feel superior to the blacks? But when we began to talk, I realized that deep inside they were not happy about the way the black man was treated in their homeland.

" It's so easy for you foreigners to criticize us," one of them said. " But if you had to live together with coloured people you'd probably treat them the same way as we do . . ."

I could feel my face getting hotter and hotter. How right they were! Back home in Europe we pat ourselves on the back, complacent in the belief that we are better than the whites who oppress the coloured peoples in various parts of the world. But even the most liberal Europeans who settle down in Africa or the East, almost invariably take the side of the local whites. It has happened in Kenya, in Algeria and in many other places. It shocks us—but what we con-demn is really something found deep inside all of us; an unconscious belief that the white man is superior, that no other civilization is equal to ours. Back home we are not forced to show our true colours—we only know the problem in theory, and then it is so easy to be idealistic . . .

And what about myself? I was no better than the two Americans, or I would have protested when the negroes went outside to make room for us. It had seemed quite reasonable to me, in fact, because I was white.

Suddenly I got up. When I went outside I nearly stumbled over the crew members who were sleeping on the deck. They had pulled a canvas cover over themselves, for the night air was raw and clammy. I shone my flashlight on them until I

found the cook. Two of them might as well sleep in my bunk,
I said when I had shaken him awake. I didn't mind sleeping
out here.

He blinked sleepily. Then a smile spread across his black,
friendly face.

" We don't mind lying out here," he said. " Don't worry
about us, we are used to a rough life. You go back in and
sleep, sir."

He pulled the canvas cover over his head. I returned to
my bunk, but it was a long time before I fell asleep. When I
woke up it looked as if two balls of fire were hanging in the
eastern horizon. It was the sun mirrored in the calm water.
" It's going to be hot," the cook said when he served us our
coffee.

I would like to have visited several of the little islands which
we sailed by during the day. One, called St. Martin, had
been half French, half Dutch since one day in 1648 when a
Frenchman and a Dutchman divided it in a rather unusual
way. After a good lunch they started a race along the beach,
but in opposite directions. The border was then drawn across
the island from their point of parting to the point where they
met again on the other side. The Frenchman was lighter on
his feet, so the Tricolor came to wave over the larger part of
the island, but the Dutchman got the most fertile land.

The engineer on the *Christine* was from Guadeloupe, the
largest of the French sugar islands in the Caribbean. He told
me that once in the sixteenth century the British had offered
Canada in exchange for Guadeloupe, but the French said,
" No, thanks "—the fertile island was considered far more
valuable than the wilderness on the North American continent!

Despite many warnings, the two Americans sunbathed for

hours in the stern. They were as red as a couple of boiled lobsters in the afternoon when we passed not far from Berbuda. This is a tiny island which William III of England presented to one of his generals. The latter, apparently not satisfied with his income from growing sugar, started a stud farm of negro slaves. The population there in those days is said to have consisted of some five hundred comely negro wenches and a small group of strong men.

" Not bad to have been one of them, eh?" said the cook, who had come over to talk to me while the others were playing cards. He told me about his childhood home on another island and about his experiences as a sailor, but most of all about his girl friends. When we came to Antigua, which was our first port of call, he was really going " to jump," he assured me. That is the West Indian expression for dancing and painting the town red.

Could I join him? His first surprise at my question was quickly replaced by a smile. Yes, with pleasure, if I really cared to!

It was nearly dark when we sailed into the little harbour, past the rusty guns of an old Portuguese fort. Along the white beach lay several luxury hotels, and further inland we could see many low, round towers. They were old windmills which had once been used to grind the juice out of the sugar cane.

Today it hardly pays to raise sugar, so many of the fields have been taken over by weeds, but the island has a new source of income which overshadows all others; the tourists. Not just the American travel-now-pay-later tours which swarm over the islands during the summer season. They help to fill the coffers too, of course, but what really keeps Antigua going is the world's biggest millionaire club, started some ten years ago on the northernmost and prettiest part of the island.

The club has approximately one hundred members, and annually they spend about half a million American dollars on the island. Each member has a private bungalow, and the golf course is said to be the finest in the West Indies.

When the crew went ashore they were almost unrecognizable in long trousers, white shirts and tennis shoes. Together with the cook I went down the badly-lit main street between two rows of low wooden houses. A crashing noise of drums and saxophones greeted us when we entered a dance hall. Many people looked at me in surprise, presumably because I was the only European in the crowded room.

The cook seemed very proud to have me with him. Every time he saw someone he knew he waved him over and told him to shake hands with me. Once or twice I tried to pay for a round of drinks, but he held my arm in a grip of steel. This was his evening!

West Indian rum is good and cheap and we were thirsty after the voyage. We both became quite hoarse, for we talked incessantly and it was difficult to make oneself heard above the din of the music. We must have sworn everlasting friendship for the third or fourth time, when he spotted a former sweetheart. They both screamed with joy, and as soon as she had been introduced and served with a glass of rum, they began to dance.

" Now it's your turn!" the cook shouted when they returned to our table, beaded with perspiration. " Come on, man—let's see what you're worth!"

The girl was cute and full of rhythm, but we northern Europeans are better at controlled and formal dances. After trying for a couple of minutes, I thanked the girl and sat down. The cook stared at me.

" I just can't," I said apologetically.

" Try again. Just relax, man ! "

I shook my head. The cook whispered something to the girl, who hid her face in her hands and giggled. " Let's finish our drinks, " he said to me, rising. " Now we're going down to the beach to have some fun. "

He put one arm around my shoulder, the other around the girl's waist, and we reeled down the road. She was a really hot girl, the cook whispered to me, and she would do it for nothing because I was his friend.

I stopped. They had better go alone and then I would wait for them at the bar, I said. He laughed and pulled my arm. Don't be shy, he said, but suddenly his smile faded.

" It's because she is black ! " he shouted. I protested vigorously, but he continued : " Yes, and that's why you wouldn't dance with her ! You people are always afraid of losing your dignity—you are afraid of being like us because we are un-civilized ! "

He staggered on with the girl. " You are all like that ! " he hurled after me. Sadly I returned to the bar. How difficult it is to build a bridge between black and white, I thought, and ordered a rum.

CHAPTER NINE

THE CANNIBAL KING

EARLY ONE MORNING the schooner chugged into a small harbour at the foot of a rugged mountain. We had reached Dominica, the most primitive of all the Caribbean islands. According to one story, when the King of Spain asked Columbus how the island looked, he crumpled a piece of paper into a ball and threw it on the table.

" Like this, Your Majesty," he replied, and as I stood at the stern of the *Christine* and looked at the wild mountains I could think of no better description.

Some historians believe Dominica was also the first place where Columbus met resistance from the natives. On the islands further north, which the Spaniards had first discovered, they had been kindly received by the small, bronzed Arawak Indians, who seemed quite unacquainted with the art of war; they only possessed light weapons for hunting.

But when the Spaniards went ashore on Dominica they were set upon by a host of well-armed warriors with pale yellowish skins and Mongolian features. Though his men had to take to their heels and several were seriously wounded, Columbus was nevertheless pleased. He thought he had encountered the vanguard of the Great Mogul and was now firmly convinced that it was really India he had discovered.

The Cannibal King

But the Spaniards soon found that, apart from the high cheekbones and slightly slanting eyes, the fierce warriors had nothing in common with the Mongols. They were roving hunters who, a few years earlier, had made their way to the islands from the South American continent. Since then they had literally lived on the Arawak Indians. In their long canoes they sailed from island to island, killing and eating the male inhabitants, for human flesh was their favourite dish. They married the Arawak women and made them grow yams with which they liked to supplement their protein diet.

For two centuries after the arrival of Columbus, the white settlers fought the cannibals, who were called Caribs, the whole area later being named after them. The Caribs never harmed women and children and when the English governor of Antigua in 1640 was carried away, together with his wife and two daughters, only he was eaten.

The Caribs also ate each other. A book written by a Dutch traveller some two hundred years ago described a party where a captured Carib witnessed the preparations for the meal of which he himself was to be the main dish. He, too, was given a cup of the home-brewed wine which the participants drank to whet their appetites.

When the fire was ready, however, tactlessly he commenced to deride the others. His family had eaten so many of them that they would practically be eating themselves, he said. A blow on the head with a club shut his mouth for ever, but the diners' mood had been spoiled and they ate the man in stony silence.

Another book written by an Englishman towards the close of the seventeenth century contains a section about the culinary art of the Caribs. The victims were first stuffed with various spices, then roasted on a spit over a slow fire. What the Caribs could not consume on the spot they smoked or salted down, so very little was wasted.

The author spent a jolly afternoon with an old, stark naked Carib woman, who showed her friendly gestures towards him by offering him a smoked arm. With a candour typical of her people she pointed out that it was no real titbit, as it was the arm of an Englishman. Arawaks and Caribs were delicious, she said, and Frenchmen nothing to sniff at, Dutchmen could just pass, but Englishmen were definitely below the mark, and Spaniards were almost inedible.

The Caribs continued to be a threat until the British decided in 1796 to remove them forcibly from the Caribbean area. The majority of them were probably killed during the ensuing manhunt. Some avoided falling into the hands of the whites by jumping off a mountain ledge which is still called "Leaper's Bluff." Eventually, some five thousand Caribs were captured and shipped to an island off British Honduras.

A small group of them survived on Dominica, where the rugged terrain made it impossible to hunt them down. As soon as the *Christine* had heaved to I went ashore and got hold of a taxi-driver. Could he take me to the Carib reservation?

I had come to the right man, replied the driver, a tall, slightly foppish negro with gleaming white teeth. He was married to the sister of the Carib King, so if anyone had close connections with the Caribs it was he. I had to be prepared to use my legs, however, as the reserve was several miles from the motor road.

Before setting off we bought provisions for the trip from a small store owned by the driver and his wife. The moment I saw her my scepticism about her royal blood was gone. She had a fair skin, Asiatic features and a quiet, dignified air;

but the most striking thing about her was her long, black hair.

"See—it is quite smooth," the driver said admiringly, stroking it gently. She smiled lovingly at him.

When the car had been filled with petrol, he poured a mug of rum down his throat. "I have to have fuel, too," he said with a laugh. My nervousness as to how this would affect his driving soon disappeared, for he manœuvred the car along the narrow mountain road with great dexterity. Soon we were up in the cool air. The sultry little capital with its monotonous huts now looked quite attractive, but perhaps that was because I could not smell it.

The driver's name was L'Homme—*The Man*—and he seemed to deserve it. Though only twenty-five years of age he had eleven illegitimate children and paid the eleven mothers eight shillings a month each towards their maintenance. This was a relatively inexpensive pleasure, and he had planned to remain a bachelor for ever, until he met the Princess. Her family had opposed the marriage, as the Caribs do not like negroes. But when the Carib King realized that it was a case of true love, he restored her to favour, and now he got along splendidly with his brother-in-law.

After an hour's drive we parked the car by the roadside and continued on foot. We carried our shoes as we were constantly wading across streams. The swift current seemed to dig the sand away from under our feet. Once I stopped and sniffed. The sweetish scent seemed familiar. It was vanilla, L'Homme told me, pointing at a green creeper which was growing up a big tree in zigzag fashion.

During the next few minutes he showed me a wild coffee bush and a cocoa bush, a coconut palm, a banana tree, an orange tree, and several kinds of edible yams which fought for space with lush sugar canes. Anything could grow in Dominica's black earth, but what was the use? It was impossible to get the produce to a market. The whole island was served by only one road, the one we had come along. Many of the inhabitants, the great majority of whom were black, lived in isolated, self-supporting communities.

The tourists were one of the few sources of cash income. They came to see the Caribs, but on hearing how far one had to walk, many lost interest and contented themselves with photographing two old Indian women who had settled down on the outskirts of the capital.

Which tourists did he prefer? The French, who often came here from nearby Guadeloupe and Martinique, were the best dressed and most polite, L'Homme replied, but they were on the whole quite stingy. The Americans were extremely generous, but dressed deplorably and easily became rude. One had called him a dirty nigger, but had given him a twenty-dollar tip. It was a difficult choice!

The new nations of Africa did not interest him in the least. His eyes were on Europe, especially Paris, and the United States. When I asked him if he knew anything about Communism, he nodded. In Martinique, where he went once a year to buy new clothes, he had met several Communists.

Their programme did not appeal to him. They wanted to take from the white and give to the black, which was all right, though it should be done with moderation lest the tourists stay away. But they also wanted to do away with God, which he found deplorable, for he loved God above everything else. And not without reason—just listen!

Until a couple of years ago L'Homme had been the owner of a popular cabaret on the outskirts of town. There had been garlands of coloured lights festooning the garden, and he also had some rooms to let by the hour. His enemies, envious of his success, had conspired against him and had him declared bankrupt just because he owed some quite insignificant sums of money. The banks had refused to help him and he could not borrow money privately at less than ten per cent per month.

Finally his cabaret had been auctioned away for a mere song. For a time he had been so down and out that he had even thought of emigrating to England. One night, overcome with despair, he had thrown himself on his knees and prayed for help. God had answered him by telling him to go to an old lady he knew and to ask her for a loan.

This he did, and she had at once agreed to lend him the sum he asked for. With the money he had been able to buy the car, pay the marriage-price for the Princess and also open the store, which, by the way, he did not intend to keep. He wanted to become a politician—which was undoubtedly the best line a smart man could take these days. The nearly three thousand inhabitants of the reservation had recently been given the right to vote, and with the Princess as a campaign asset, he was a sure winner.

" Now do you understand why I love my God?" he asked, with a bright smile which disarmed me completely.

On a muddy hillside we met the first Caribs, two young women and a boy who nodded in reply to L'Homme's hearty greetings. Each one carried a basket of bananas which they were planning to sell to passers-by on the road. They had high cheekbones, but the boy and one of the girls had brown skin and slightly curly hair. Shyly they smiled at me and agreed to let me photograph them. When I gave them a bottle of soda water to share, the light-skinned girl removed the crown top with her teeth.

Among themselves they spoke a *patois*—the island had been French until the British took it during the French revolution —but they also knew a little English. This they had learned from an Irish priest who said Mass at the reservation every other week.

There were only about a hundred pure Caribs left, L'Homme told me as we walked on. The rest of the inhabitants of the reservation had a little African blood in their veins. Only the mixed-bloods left the reservation to earn money—no true Carib would work for someone else.

This tallied with what I had read about the Carib way of life in the old days. They never became slaves and those who, from time to time, had agreed to serve the whites had never kept the jobs for long. At the slightest reprimand they would run away or eat earth until they died from it—which, curiously enough, was their favourite method of committing suicide.

To Christianize them had demanded a great deal of patience. Despite diligent missionary work, not a single Carib was converted during the first hundred years after the arrival of the whites. In those days, however, a small group of them made a living by sailing from island to island and letting themselves be baptized. The missionaries, delighted finally to be able to save some Carib souls, rewarded them with presents, whereupon they would sail on to the next island.

The Caribs had no word for God, soul or spirit. So it is not surprising that they had difficulty in grasping the Christian dogmas. They acknowledged a difference between good and evil, but when they sacrificed occasionally, it was only to the evil elements, which they respected because they could do them harm.

It is said that only the men understood the Carib tongue

and kept it secret from the women, who spoke Arawak among themselves. The men pretended not to understand this language although they had all learned it during childhood.

Most travellers who visited the Caribs were struck by the difference in temperaments betwen the men and the women. The women often smiled and sang, whereas the men went about in sullen silence, or just sat around the fires and stared into nothingness. They seem to have had an almost unlimited capacity for idling their time away. When one occasionally spoke, the others would give a slight nod. It never occurred to them to interrupt and they nod although the speaker might express an opinion quite the opposite to their own.

They seldom quarrelled among themselves, but at drinking parties a man might sneak up behind someone against whom he had a grudge, bash his head in with a stroke of a club, and return to his place. The others would pretend that nothing had happened, but it was not unlikely that at the next party the relatives of the murdered man would take revenge.

In those days the Caribs had no chiefs. The custom of electing a King began only about half a century ago when the British insisted upon them having a leader to facilitate the administration of the reservation. The old Caribs looked with contempt at the class structure of the white people. As far as they were concerned no man with any self-respect would dream of obeying anybody else. The decision to go on the warpath was usually reached during a drinking bout—someone would begin to talk about how this or that enemy had insulted them, whereupon they would all jump up, grab their arms and run to the boats.

They were, and still are, excellent sailors. L'Homme said that the Caribs sometimes paddle as far as Puerto Rico or Cuba in their little boats. The main purpose of these voyages is to smuggle liquor. They have to make a living somehow, and tilling the soil has never really appealed to them.

This I had surmised when we had passed several of their fields. Like many primitive Indians of South America, they just burn off the trees and bushes on a slope and plant yams in the ashes. After a couple of years the field is ruined by erosion and they burn off a new area.

I was nearly worn out when, after a couple of hours of climbing up steep mountain sides, we reached the King's hut, which was standing on stilts in a clearing. In the doorway sat a naked light-skinned child whose swollen stomach showed that he probably had worms. At the sight of us the child made an exclamation and a barefooted young man came out.

One could easily have taken him for a Chinese as he stood there in the sun, blinking his almond-shaped eyes. He was the King of the Caribs. Somehow I had a feeling that he did not really look at me. But how could I expect that when I had two cameras with lenses gleaming like evil eyes, dangling round my neck?

Noisily L'Homme introduced us to each other. The King then asked if I wanted to photograph him, adding politely that it would cost me a dollar. When I nodded, he disappeared into the hut and returned, wearing shoes and a jacket. Over one shoulder he had a broad ribbon and he was leaning on a silver-knobbed walking stick. The stick was the sceptre of the Caribs, a present from a King of England.

Erect and solemn, he stood in front of the little hut while I was busy photographing him. When I had finished he took off his shoes and jacket and invited us inside the narrow room which was furnished with a low table and two benches. On the wall was a picture of Queen Elizabeth and Prince Philip and a colour photo of our host in full regalia. The latter

Trinidad has an extremely mixed population, but the negro blood predominates.

14. Christmas in Trinidad's "shanty-town". Some of the guests hid a broadsword beneath their clothes. When the dancing started they stripped to the skin.

5. Cheddi Jagan explaining his ideas to Chi-yun. "I am a Marxist", he said. He feels convinced that the best way of solving the problems of the undeveloped countries will be planned economy. Cheddi Jagan is a great admirer of Castro, but would prefer to use democratic means when carrying through his "revolution" in Guiana. However, much seems to indicate that the opposition will not allow this.

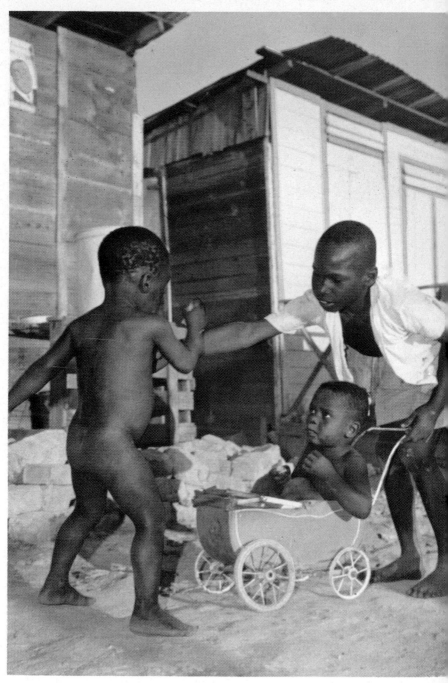

16. During the years of slavery family feeling was systematically killed among the negroes. The children grow up without traditions and without any kind of discipline.

turned out to be a postcard. " To our friend, the Carib King with best regards," I read on the other side. " Sincerely yours, Mr. and Mrs. K. T. Smith, Toledo, Ohio."

We must be hungry after the long walk, the King said in his slow and careful English, adding that I was welcome to have some Carib food. He must have expected a refusal, for he looked at me in surprise when I said that I would love some. L'Homme slapped me on the back and shouted approvingly that I sure didn't stick up my nose at native food. The King gave an order to his sister, a young and pronouncedly pregnant woman, who was the mother of the child with the swollen tummy. She went to the kitchen, which was in a nearby hut, and soon smoke came pouring out of the door.

I tried to learn a little about the young King, but though he answered my questions politely enough I never had any feeling of real contact with him. Perhaps that would be too much to ask when one comes dashing up on a three-hour visit. He had attended the reservation school here until he was fifteen. Then he had spent four years at a boarding school in the capital of Dominica and had only returned here a few months ago.

Where did he prefer to live? " Here," he replied. In town there were too many people and everyone was very busy.

Shortly after his return the election for a King, which was held every five years, had come due. All adults had the right to vote, but there was no election campaign—that was only permitted at the island-wide elections. He had been an easy winner because he had had a better education than any other Carib.

What were his royal duties? To mediate when people were at odds with one another and to pass final judgment if they could not reach an agreement. Before doing so he would ask the advice of the old people who knew the unwritten laws of the Caribs. Criminal cases had to be handed over to the island authorities, but that was hardly ever necessary. Disagreements were usually caused by petty thieving. The Caribs had formerly lived in large family groups, owning most things in common, and they had never really learned to respect the individual's property rights.

The school also came under the King's jurisdiction, and he had to see to it that the old and weak received a pension amounting to about eight shillings a month per person. He himself received an annual salary of £32 sterling—too little, he thought, for as King he did not have much time left for growing yams and had to buy most of his foodstuffs. That was why he had to charge for being photographed.

I was anxious to hear some Carib, but the King could not speak it. Only the old people still remembered a few words, he said. Strangely enough, the language is still kept alive by the thirty thousand descendants of the Caribs in British Honduras, although they are so mixed with the local negroes that they can hardly be told apart from them.

Did the King intend to get married? No, he replied. There were no suitable Carib girls of his age. By " suitable " he undoubtedly meant girls of pure blood.

I was ravenously hungry when the food finally was ready. I had heard that the Caribs were fond of fish, which is also my favourite food, but to my disappointment we were served dried codfish which had come all the way from Norway! To the West Indians, imported fish is so much finer than fresh fish, L'Homme explained. Altogether, no local goods can compete with foreign ones. The dried cod was fried in oil with yams, a kind of spinach and with lots of pepper. It tasted very good, although the fish was a bit tough.

The Cannibal King

It was nearly impossible to walk in the mountains after dark, so we had to take our leave as soon as we had finished eating. When we were alone again I said sadly to L'Homme that the pure Caribs would soon die out. Yes, but he did not think that was worth worrying about as most of them were weak and lacked initiative. They needed fresh blood and he was helping to supply just that! His wife was already pregnant and the Caribs would live on in the future little L'Homme and many other strong mixtures. They would be darker than the Caribs, but this he considered an advantage, for he found white skin strangely cold. The one thing he regretted was the loss of their smooth hair—it was so pretty, he concluded, running a hand over his own kinky head.

CHAPTER TEN

THE REDLEGS

BARBADOS IS ONE of Britain's oldest colonies, and the many years under British rule have somehow made it resemble the mother country. Here is no tropical wilderness. Everything on the flat island, which measures twenty-one miles by fourteen, is tamed and orderly. Between the regular green fields lie old manor houses built in Tudor style. Instead of the usual jumble of corrugated iron sheds, the towns consist of solid stone houses grouped around old churches.

Some find Barbados boring just because it is so much like England, but I was eager to get ashore when the *Christine* arrived there one day, shortly before noon. I had read that on this island one still finds descendants of a group of white convicts who came to the West Indies at the time of Cromwell. " Redlegs," they were called, presumably because their legs were burned by the sun when they worked in the fields. For hundreds of years they lived under the same conditions as the negro slaves. Had this changed them, and how did they now manage compared to the blacks? That was what I wanted to find out.

Barbados is one of the most popular holiday resorts in the Caribbean, and the harbour was so crowded with yachts that there was hardly room for the *Christine*. As soon as we had heaved to I went up the cosy little main street which had the atmosphere of a large English village. It annoyed me a bit that there were so many people who, like myself, carried cameras around their necks. Tourists are never very happy at the sight of other tourists, I am afraid.

The first policeman I came across was standing in front of a statue of Lord Nelson, looking exactly like a London bobby, except that he was black. When I asked where I could find some "redlegs," he replied in a strong Scottish accent that as far as he knew there were some living in the county of St. John. I could go there by a number four bus. It started from the next corner—and I should get off at the church on the hill . . .

"Thank you," I said and hurried on, for there was not much time to be lost as the *Christine* was leaving again in the evening. In the bus I happened to occupy a seat next to the only other white passenger, a middle-aged man whom I immediately guessed to be English. Who else would be wearing a flannel blazer in this heat?

We quickly started a conversation, and it turned out that he was indeed an Englishman, but had been born in *Barrrr-bados* as he pronounced it—like the policeman, he rolled his r's. He was a travelling salesman in agricultural machinery. A couple of days ago his car had broken down in the country, and now he was going back to pick it up at the garage.

I explained my errand and asked if he could tell me anything about the "redlegs." "Not much," he replied. There were a few hundred of them left, but he did not know any personally as they lived in small, isolated communities. The history of the island had always interested him, however, so he knew a little about their background.

In the beginning of the seventeenth century, many whites

had come to Barbados as bondsmen to work for a certain number of years, usually ten. Their master was obliged to pay their passage and to give them a small piece of land at the end of their term of service.

It is hard to understand that anyone would sell ten years of life for a ticket to Barbados, but in those days the lower classes in England were very badly off. Shortly before, the landed gentry had given up raising grain in favour of keeping sheep. One herdsman replaced about a dozen day-labourers and the unemployed streamed to the cities. But here they could not find work either—the Industrial Revolution was yet to come.

The new West Indian colony actually had a bad name because so many who went there succumbed to fever. " Go to Barbados " was then the equivalent of wishing someone to perdition. The fact that so many came was due, more than anything else, to the promise of a piece of land of their own. The displaced farmhands were just as hungry for land as they were for food . . .

The bus started and from the narrow main street we quickly reached the countryside. When we drove between the fields our view was cut off by the arm-thick stalks of sugar cane which waved gently in the breeze, but there was seldom more than a few minutes between the villages, which were alive with people, most of them blacks. With its 250,000 inhabitants Barbados is, after the Yangtze valley, the most densely populated area in the world. There is no industry to speak of, and one wonders how so many can live off so little land. Without the income from the tourists it would probably not be possible.

I asked the Englishman to continue. He told me that immediately on their arrival the bondsmen were usually auctioned away to impoverished estate owners who could not afford to invest in negro slaves. A black cost more than twice as much as a white man, and apart from being able to work harder in the tropical climate, the negro was almost immune to the fever.

The first year was the most dangerous one for the whites. If they were still alive at the end of it their value would rise by more than one third. The chance that they would survive their period of service was still slight, however. The owner, eager to keep the piece of land which was due to his bondsman, would try to squeeze the utmost possible work out of him on the least possible food. It was a race between freedom and death.

Even those who won the race became losers in the last instance. With the rising prices of land, the estate owners soon succeeded in getting a law passed which made it legal for them to give a bondsman four hundred pounds of sugar instead of the piece of land. If the bondsman sold the sugar he would not even receive sufficient money for a ticket home. Free men were not wanted as workers on the plantations, and many had to bind themselves again in order not to starve to death.

Some ran away before their term of service had expired and hid in the forests which in those days were still to be found on the island. Here they stayed in caves and lived by hunting, supplemented with what they could steal from the fields. Their number increased rapidly under Cromwell, who used Barbados as a kind of dumping ground. Many a refractory Scot or Irishman was exiled to the island, and after a clean-up of the slums of London, one ship after another arrived with robbers, murderers and prostitutes. They were all sold on arrival, but many escaped from the plantations and joined the outlaws in the forest who finally numbered several thousand.

119

Revolt in the Tropics

Many times there was talk of exterminating them, but early in the eighteenth century the estate owners changed their minds. Due to the heavy import of negro slaves, the population of the island, which had at first been nearly white, was now predominantly black. After two negro revolts, which were suppressed with difficulty, the landowners were ordered to put one white soldier at the disposal of the authorities for every twenty-five acres of land they possessed.

But where should the soldiers come from? To ship them out from England would be far too expensive. There were none to be hired locally—or were there? What about the redlegs? They were becoming a danger in themselves, and if they could be used against the negroes, two birds would be killed with one stone! If you dangled a piece of land in front of their noses, they would surely return to the fold.

The plan succeeded. The outlaws were drawn back into the community, though not as equals of the other white citizens. They were not allowed to vote, and they were only given land as a loan and on the condition that they worked for the estate owners for a part of the year.

" In a way they were worse off than when they were bondsmen," my English informant said. " They were no longer masters of their own time, but now they had to feed themselves. This was difficult for them, since they were given the poorest land and they had never learned to cultivate the earth properly. My grandmother told me that many of them begged from the blacks, who despised them. ' Poor whites ' they called them—and that is still one of the most offensive expressions one can use here."

When slavery was abolished towards the middle of the last century, the redlegs were freed from doing villein service, and later on they acquired the right to vote, but this did not bring about any real improvement in their conditions. The redlegs, however, were far from being the only Barbadians who lived in poverty. Most of the small farmers suffered from the unequal distribution of land. It had been calculated that five acres were the minimum on which a family could live, but four-fifths of the farmers had only about one acre and that was usually rented land.

Then how could they manage? They worked on the plantations, or at the hotels during the tourist season, but it was not always easy to find a job. Like everywhere else in the Caribbean, there was a great deal of unemployment outside the harvest season . . .

The bus stopped in front of a lovely old church on the top of a hill. I waved goodbye to the pleasant Englishman and started walking along a side road which wound its way down the hill. Chirping birds flitted in and out of the sugar cane which rose like a wall on either side. It was like walking alone in a forest, but after some minutes I heard voices. They came from a small shop which was near the road, opposite three shacks.

My entry into the shop was followed by a sudden silence. Apart from the shopkeeper and his wife, who were standing behind the counter, there were five barefooted and very poorly dressed people in the little room. Though pretending not to see me they all watched me closely. I wondered whether they were sisters and brothers, for all had the same yellowish-white hair, washed-out blue eyes and long, bony faces with weak chins.

After many years as a travelling reporter I have come to regard myself as something of an expert in making contacts with people, but here I failed to make any headway. They did not seem in the least interested when I told them that I was a journalist and very anxious to learn something about their way of life. My offer of a bottle of lemonade or a cigarette was curtly refused.

When I had smoked and drunk for a moment in icy silence I opened my camera bag. This often calls forth comment which leads on to a conversation, but I could not discern even a glimmer of curiosity in their rabbit-like eyes. In desperation I set off my flash. They did not so much as blink.

Crestfallen, I paid and went outside. Immediately the hum of voices began again. From habit I took out my notebook to put down my first impressions while they were still fresh in my mind. " Redlegs not friendly towards strangers," I wrote.

It was already getting late in the afternoon. Did I really have to return to the *Christine* without having achieved my object? My glance fell on the nearest one of the three huts, and stopped there. Half a dozen children were staring at me from an open window. Their eyes were also light-coloured, but they were not in the least unfriendly. I approached gingerly as if afraid to frighten away a flock of birds.

" What is your name?" I asked the biggest one, a girl with thin plaits. They were all quite dirty and dressed in worn, faded clothes.

" Belinda Gibson," she replied with the same Scottish accent I had heard in town. Were they alone in the house? No, mom and granny were in the kitchen. Could I talk to them? They disappeared into a back room, and a moment later the whole flock came galloping back, followed by a wrinkled, almost toothless woman wearing a ragged cotton dress. Before she opened the door I saw her stick her naked feet into a pair of worn tennis shoes. I had a feeling that she did not really understand me when I explained that I was a journalist, but she asked me inside just the same.

The room contained nothing but a sofa with a worn cover, four rickety chairs, a clock that had stopped and a lot of dirty clothes. Even so it gave an impression of confusion, perhaps due to the many children who were in constant motion. How many were there altogether?

"Twelve," replied the old lady, whose name was Charlotte Gibson. She sat down in the sofa, and at once they were crawling all around her, struggling to get on her lap. They were her grandchildren—a wild, unruly flock, she added with a sigh, putting her arms around them like a mother hen. She herself had brought nine children into the world, but only three were still living, a son and two daughters. The son was working in the fields, the younger daughter was in town where she had a job at a laundry, and the other daughter was busy in the kitchen.

How much land did they own? None at all. They rented five acres for three dollars a month (a West Indian dollar is equal to about four shillings). In a good year they could harvest fifteen tons of cane which they sold for about fourteen dollars a ton, but transport expenses swallowed a good deal of the money. Her son occasionally found work at the plantations, but their only steady income was the younger daughter's weekly wage of twelve dollars. It wasn't much when you had so many mouths to feed.

"But we manage," she added with sudden Anglo-Saxon dignity. "We don't complain."

Would she show me the rest of the house? Yes, but I had to walk carefully as some of the floorboards were rotten. The house did not belong to them either; they rented it for three dollars a month, and the owner refused to make any repairs.

Apart from the sitting-room there was a small bedroom with two beds in which the four grown-ups slept, while the children

lay on the floor. The kitchen, a crude lean-to, was so leaky
that I could see the sky through the roof. At the open fire-
place a pregnant woman was stirring the contents of a cooking
pot. There was something inexpressibly tired about the pale,
thin face and the greyish eyes that looked at me from deep
sockets. Sitting astride her hip was a brown-skinned boy with
curly hair.

I wanted very much to take some pictures before the sun
disappeared, so Olinda, as she was called, took the pot off
the fire and went out into the muddy backyard with us. The
bright daylight revealed that they all had little festering
wounds on their arms and legs. Every time they moved,
clouds of tiny insects would rise from the inflamed spots.

Back in the sitting-room I asked Mrs. Gibson where her
ancestors came from. Probably Scotland or Ireland, she replied without any interest, and she had no idea how long
her family had been on the island. She was born just beyond
the hill in 1920 . . .

I gave a start. I had thought of her as an old woman—
and she was more than a year younger than I! How old was
Olinda? "Twenty-one," the pale young woman replied,
stroking her child's curly hair.

Mrs. Gibson noticed that I glanced wonderingly at the
flock of children. "We start early here," she said with a little
smile. "I was married to Mr. Gibson when I was fourteen. He
was a man of honour, bless his soul never touched a drink in
all his life, but my daughters haven't been so lucky. Olinda
had her first one when she was thirteen, by a useless fellow
who never sent a penny to help support the child. The others
don't either, at least not regularly—none except the father
of this little darling."

She took the brown child from her daughter and kissed his

124

cheek tenderly. "Was the father a white man?" I asked, turning red in the face. How I hated asking the question. They seemed to find it quite natural, however. "No, he was coloured," Mrs. Gibson replied. When she was a child she had received a beating if she so much as talked to a negro, but times had changed. Now it was not considered shameful to have a child by a negro, and the truth was that many of the coloured people were much better than the whites. They were not so calculating and deceitful.

Had they never thought of emigrating? Mrs. Gibson shook her head slowly. They had heard of people who went to England or Canada, but the ticket cost several hundred dollars. How could they ever put aside so much when they barely had enough to live on and often got only one meal a day? No, they could never get away from Barbados . . .

I left soon after. The curse that hung over many of the former slaves also seemed to extend to the "redlegs," I thought as I made my way up the hill. Both had had their chains removed more than a century ago—but since then they had been left to their own devices. Nothing had ever been done to replace the loss they had suffered when they were torn away from the culture and traditions that are the natural heritage of every people. The ignorance of the past continued to breed in them—and how was it possible to stop this vicious circle?

When I was waiting for the bus I took out my notebook and opened it on the first of the afternoon's entries. "Redlegs not friendly towards strangers," I read, and then I crossed it out.

CHAPTER ELEVEN

THE PEACE CORPS

ON THE SAILING trip from Puerto Rico to Trinidad I brought along a small guidebook entitled *The Call of the Caribbean*. Even the most fastidious tourist would not read many pages of it without yearning to go there. The author describes the islands as " a string of pearls," and their inhabitants as " carefree children of nature who sing and dance under swaying palms in the cool tropical night."

But when he came to St. Lucia, a large and rather mountainous island in the south-eastern Caribbean Sea, he had evidently run out of adjectives. He dismisses it as " beautiful," adding for historical background that St. Lucia holds two West Indian records. The French captured the island thirteen times before it finally remained under the British flag, and its capital has been burned down eight times since it was founded.

" Nothing of interest," the author concludes bluntly; so I did not expect much when, early one afternoon, I came walking down the main street which runs from the harbour to the mountains about a mile and a half inland. The architecture seemed unusually ugly even for this part of the world, with many of the houses made of cement—the inhabitants evidently had no desire to improve on the fire record.

The Peace Corps

At a crossroads a black policeman made a great to-do about directing the pedestrians and a few cyclists. When a jeep approached, he threw his head back and raised his arm—but not to let it pass. No sir, it had to stop so that everyone could see what an important fellow he was.

Noticing the words " Peace Corps " on the door of the jeep, I dashed across the street. Excuse me, but were they members of President Kennedy's Peace Corps? I asked the two young men in the front seat. Sure, they had been here for nearly six months. They lived on the other side of the island and were now going home after having done their weekly shopping.

I considered for a moment. We would be here for at least two days, the Captain of the *Christine* had said, so I had plenty of time. " May I go with you?" I asked, explaining that I was a journalist. " Sure," they replied in one voice. " Hop in. I'm Joe and this is Bill. Glad to meet you, Karl !"

Both were in shirtsleeves and wrinkled khaki trousers. Joe was a small and wiry Virginian whose quick movements contrasted strangely with his slow drawl. Bill, who was big and beefy, spoke with the nasal twang of the Middle West.

We roared past the bungalows of the local upper classes in the foothills. Here it was already a little cooler. I caught a glimpse of the *Christine,* lying at the quay like a grey beetle. When the last houses had disappeared we came to a humid forest where the creepers grew all the way to the edge of the road.

The two Americans told me that the local Peace Corps consisted of eighteen young men and women. Most of them were teachers or nurses and worked in town. Joe and Bill, who were agricultural graduates, lived in a village . . .

Suddenly Joe had to step on the brake to avoid hitting a

127

furry little animal which darted across the road. That was a mongoose, " Rikki-tikki-tavi," as Kipling called them. On some of the West Indian islands there are millions of them. They were brought here shortly after the abolition of slavery to do away with the poisonous snakes which were then a plague. It is said that the snakes had been imported too, and let loose by the planters to frighten the slaves from running away and hiding in the forests.

Whether the poisonous reptiles served their purpose is not known, but they were exterminated by the " Rikki-tikki-tavis," as was the birdlife on many of the islands. However clever the birds were at hiding their nests, the agile, furry animals would find them and eat the eggs, so the twitter of birds is seldom heard in the West Indies these days.

As we went higher up the forest thinned out and, after a while, we came to a savannah-like tableland. Here meat was cheap, Bill said, waving to a shepherd, who was tending some cattle, but a few miles away it was nearly impossible to obtain meat. There was no trade between the various districts of the island because this was virtually the only road.

We had just caught a glimpse of the sea on the other side of the island, when Joe shouted, " Hold on!" and made a sharp turn to the right. The jeep bumped down a miserable side road, and the moment we stopped on top of a hill a choking cloud of dust which the car had churned up caught up with us.

On the slope at our feet were about a dozen oblong vegetable beds with narrow ditches between them. " This is just about the only tangible result we have to show," Bill said. " It isn't much, but then it is probaby the only cultivated spot on the island where you won't find any erosion. The drainage ditches do the trick."

When the negroes had tilled a field for a couple of years, the topsoil would be washed away by the rains and they had to clear a new patch of land. At first Bill and Joe had tried to explain to them that apart from being destructive, this procedure demanded disproportionately more labour. Such theories did not make any impression on the negroes, but they did trust their own eyes. They had been impressed when they saw, after the last rainy season, that the earth had not been washed away from the fields of the Americans.

"When we heard that the first farmer had begun to dig drainage ditches, we celebrated with a bottle of rum," Joe said with a smile. "Now there are several who have started doing it."

On the drained slope they had planted half a dozen different kinds of vegetables which until then had been unknown on St. Lucia, and also several kinds of fruit trees. A few of them did not thrive in the humid heat, but most of them managed quite well.

The problem was how to get the negroes to raise them. They knew practically only yams, rice, corn and bananas—and thought that was enough. They were extremely conservative, and in Bill's opinion, this was mainly due to their poverty. When they followed the old and tried methods they knew they could just grow enough to enable them to keep body and soul together. An experiment which failed could result in starvation.

I drew a sigh of relief when Joe started the engine and turned the jeep round. When one stopped in the sun, it felt as if one was sitting under a huge burning glass. Did they not find the climate enervating? They nodded.

"If it wasn't so hot maybe it wouldn't be so difficult to make the farmers try something new," Bill said. Some of them had begun to realize that it would pay them to raise new crops such as beans and cucumbers, but no one had planted any yet.

" Several times they have asked whether we would do it for them," Bill continued. " And we did plant a small bed for a couple of them, hoping that they would go on by themselves, but afterwards they asked us to weed and water the beds for them too! It seems as if they feel that we owe them something."

Perhaps this attitude went back to the days of slavery when all initiative came from the white boss, I said. Some days ago I met an old Englishman who had told me how he once came to a negro village which was threatened by flooding. A dike had been damaged by a storm and sea water was pouring into their fields. The villagers sat on a hill, wailing.

Why didn't they do something about it, the Englishman inquired. They could easily repair the damage.

Yes, but that was hard work—you couldn't ask anyone to do it for less than a shilling an hour, and who would pay them?

The two Americans nodded thoughtfully. They had some-times come across the same attitude. Joe believed that the poor diet of the natives also had something to do with their lack of energy. A couple of months ago he had attended a soccer match between two local teams, one from a school, the other from a reformatory. Although they belonged to the same age group, the school team had been trounced by nine goals to nil.

" During the game, I talked to the teacher of the reformatory," Joe said. " He told me that the same thing happened every year and he was convinced that it was because his boys got a healthy, varied diet. Usually the negroes here get nothing but yams and rice and corn—and you can't expect such poor fuel to develop much energy, can you?"

I learned that the United States up to then had sent about a thousand Peace Corps members to a dozen different countries. All were men and women who had volunteered for a two-year period of service. The average age was about twenty-four. Before being sent abroad they had been given an eight weeks' course at a special training school established in Puerto Rico for members of the Peace Corps. Here they studied mainly languages and the historical background of the countries where they were to serve. They were also given political instruction.

" We were taught the best possible answers to many questions which the teachers thought we would be asked by Communists wanting to trip us up," Joe said. " I never had any use for those answers, fortunately. All that propaganda stuff doesn't hold with me. I joined the Peace Corps not for political reasons, but because I wanted to travel and learn something about the world."

" That goes for me too," Bill said. This attitude struck me as pleasantly free from high-flown idealism. They had gone abroad mainly for their own sake, but they also had something to give in return. This was honest trading which did not place the people in the under-developed countries in a moral debt to them.

From Puerto Rico they had gone to Trinidad to attend lecures at the University for six weeks. " That was really to teach us how to get along with people in other countries," Joe explained. " Of course you can't be taught such a thing. That would be a kind of professional salesmanship which any people would soon see through. Well, now we're home . . ."

We had come to two long rows of huts: poor dwellings, a

couple of shops, a bar and a little post office. Some distance away was a modern bungalow where the two Americans lived. As we drove up, Joe smiled apologetically. Before being sent out he had imagined a primitive camping life, he said. In a way he would have preferred to rough it, but the local Ministry of Agriculture had built the bungalow for them. Apart from free housing they received a monthly wage of about a hundred American dollars from the local authorities.

In the sitting-room, two mulattos were waiting for Joe and Bill. They were their colleagues: young officials from the Ministry of Agriculture. There was an air of easy informality between them and the two Americans. Every Peace Corps member has a local " counterpart " with whom he or she works, I now learned.

" It has its advantages," Joe told me when he and I were alone. " Of course they know a lot that we don't know, and thanks to them we avoid friction with the authorities. On the other hand it prevents us from doing very much independent work."

I was put up on the sofa, and Joe's counterpart, who was going to town the next day, promised to give me a lift back. After dinner, Joe and I went for a walk in the village. The faces of the negroes were almost indiscernible in the darkness which prevailed outside the small islands of light under the street lamps.

Everyone shouted greetings as we walked by : " Hello, Joe! What about a glass of rum, Joe! Give me a shilling, Joe!"

He grinned. " In the beginning I was irritated by their begging, but it is just a greeting. They don't really expect anything. If you can only make them laugh it is easy to get along with them."

Some young fellows sitting in front of the post office begged a smoke from Joe. " Sit down and have a chat," they said, making room for us. Joe winked at a tall negro who wore tennis shoes; the others were barefooted.

" Well, how you doing, Frank?" he asked.

" Okay, okay, thanks to the Lord and my own moderation," Frank replied with mock seriousness. " But it would help a bit if you could give me a job, man!"

" When did you have a job last?"

" It's so long ago I can hardly remember it any more, man! But let me tell you it's hard for a man with my diligent nature to go idle!"

The others laughed noisily. The economy of the island was stagnating, and most of the men in the village were unemployed except for three or four months of the year, Joe told me. Of course the Peace Corps did some good, but what was really needed was some small industries, of which there were none at all. Where was the capital to come from? Apart from the few islands favoured by the tourists, the West Indian islands were not considered a good area of investment.

" When I first came here the poverty used to depress me," he continued. " The negroes here have no possibility of improving their lot. They can't emigrate either . . ."

He stopped to listen. From the darkness came a delicate tinkling, as if from a xylophone. " Come on," he said, rising. " Now we're going to have fun!"

In front of the bar a crowd had gathered around four young men, each of whom was bending over a big drum. It was the local steel band, the " Blue Devils." They had made the drums themselves by hammering round dents into one end of old oil drums. Now they were tuning them by giving each dent a work-over with a stone.

" Okay, boys," the leader said, and then " Silent Night "

sprang from the primitive musical instruments. I had never before seen anyone dance to it except round the Christmas tree back in Scandinavia, but here they commenced without hesitation. In a few minutes the street was full of singing, twisting and rocking negroes. Without being directed by anyone, they formed a line behind the four drummers who moved slowly down the street, with the drums hanging from straps around their necks.

A girl whose kinky hair formed a dark halo around her head came over to Joe and put her arm around his waist. " That's right, man!" someone shouted as the American hurled himself into a wild dance with her. A moment later I felt myself seized by a pair of strong arms.

" Dance with me," a husky female voice whispered into my ear as I was pressed against a large, warm bosom. I had been captured by Anita, a happy young girl with jutting buttocks.

Someone or other handed us a bottle of home-brewed rum which was going from hand to hand. Quickly I took a second sip to extinguish the fire in my throat. Anita moved a couple of steps away from me and, raising her skirts, came slowly towards me as she moved her hips back and forth with rhythmical thrusts. I stopped, shocked.

" Come on, man!" Joe shouted. " Do it too—don't be a prude!"

Now I saw that all the girls had raised their skirts and were dancing towards their partners who were also shaking their hips, shouting with joy. Suddenly I realized that there was nothing indecent about the dance, it was my way of looking at it that was wrong. With a feeling of relief I began to sway my hips in time with the music.

Twice we danced to the end of the main street and back. Then Joe and I went into the bar and cooled off with a beer.

Joe nodded when I told him that it was a long time since I had enjoyed myself so much. Though he had lived among negroes all his life he had never really known any until he came to St. Lucia.

" It's amusing to think that I used to have all sorts of ideas about saving them," he said, smiling as he shook his head. " In fact I've learned more from them than they have from me. I never knew how to relax and be myself until I came here. They are poor, but in a way they're the happiest people I've ever known."

He emptied his glass. Outside, the drums had started on " Old Man River." The negroes were still dancing.

CHAPTER TWELVE

POTPOURRI

TAKE FOUR PARTS negro and three parts Indian, add one part Chinese and a dash of Frenchman, Syrian and Englishman. Stir well under a burning tropical sun . . .

That is more or less the recipe used by fate and British colonialism in producing the population of Trinidad. What a mess, some will probably think, but people with a yen for spicy things become extremely fond of the island and its colourful inhabitants.

When I went there to meet Chi-yun, it was with the intention of staying only a few days. We remained there for more than a month, and if we ever return to the West Indies it will be to revisit this island.

It is less than two thousand square miles in area, but is richly endowed by nature. On the fertile coastal plains, cultivated plants shoot forth as though in a hothouse. The mountains, from which one can see the mainland of South America, are covered with cool forests. Beneath it all are huge stores of oil which supply the government with more than half its income and make Trinidad much wealthier than the surrounding islands.

Another seemingly inexhaustible source of income is the famous pitch lake. It is hard to imagine a more dreary sight than this hundred-acre field of black pitch which has supplied asphalt for the roads of the world ever since the invention of the automobile. Although millions of tons of the viscous mass have been removed, there seems to be nearly as much as ever : the surface of the lake has sunk by less than a foot.

Sir Walter Raleigh wrote that he used pitch from the lake for caulking his ships. He said that nowhere had he seen so many humming birds as on Trinidad; they whirred round him and his men wherever they went.

Today there are not so many of them. The tiny birds never seem to have recovered from the setback they suffered towards the close of the last century when European and American women suddenly developed a craze for ornamenting their hats with stuffed humming birds. For several years, fifteen thousand birds a week were exported from Trinidad alone.

The Spaniards were the first to occupy the island, but they never got much out of it. From the Moors, who ruled Spain for hundreds of years, the proud sons of Castile had learned to despise agriculture. They wanted gold and lost interest in the island when they realized that it did not contain much of that precious metal. A few hundred men were stationed at a naval base—Port of Spain—which was later to become the capital. On the rest of the island, the wild Caribs had more or less a free hand.

It was the negro rebellion on Haiti which really set things humming in Trinidad. A group of French planters fled to the Spanish island where they took up the struggle against the wilderness and the Caribs. They had to have labourers, so the slave ships from Africa began calling at Port of Spain.

When the island was conquered in 1802 by the English, who have kept it ever since, there were already many large plantations. The abolition of slavery in all British dependencies a few years later nearly put a stop to further development. At first the humanistic British law did not make much difference. In those days it was realized that it would not do to give the negroes complete freedom too suddenly. Instead, it was done in stages so that both the blacks and their masters could adjust themselves to the change.

Judging by the written accounts from those days, most of the negroes preferred to stay on at the plantations even after they had been granted complete freedom. They had never learned to stand on their own feet and seemed to be a little afraid of doing so.

But in 1834 this changed. On Trinidad it is still spoken of as "the year when the negroes stopped working." Why they did it just then is difficult to say. Perhaps some of them had proved to the rest that it was not so difficult to manage by yourself. All you had to do was to burn a piece of forest, plant some yams and breadfruit trees and then lie down to wait for nature to take care of the rest.

The great majority of the negroes left the plantations, and in vain the owners tried to tempt them back with good wages. After a couple of unsuccessful attempts to import workers from Madeira and the Canary Islands, the British authorities turned their attention to China. Here there were many men who were willing to go to the end of the world to get away from the famines which were always stalking the great empire.

The first gangs of indentured Chinese coolies were imported about a hundred years ago. They were to work from seven to ten years for the planters, who then had to give them a small piece of land or a passage home. Their wages were slightly more than half of what the black workers were paid. Practically no Chinese wanted to return home after the expiration of their contracts. On the contrary, they opened small shops and, when they had saved up a little money, sent for their relatives. Many a Chinese woman arriving in Trinidad discovered that since she last saw her husband, he had acquired a flock of children with slanting eyes and curly hair. Living in celibacy seldom appeals to the Chinese, so many of them had taken black concubines. Long afterwards it was common for the Chinese in Trinidad to maintain two families, one Chinese and one coloured.

The Chinese abroad have always helped each other. When the next shipment of coolies arrived, they immediately borrowed money from the newly-established Chinese merchants, bought their freedom and opened more shops. Thus the contract system primarily served to aid the poor but ambitious Chinese in getting cheap transport to the new world.

The British authorities now began to tap another reservoir of cheap labour : India. It was hoped that the Indians would stay longer in the fields, but it did not take them long to work their way up either. As soon as they could buy their freedom they began to grow rice and vegetables on their own.

When the contract system was finally dropped early in this century, it had not served its original purpose very well, but thanks to it the island had acquired a diligent community of businessmen and farmers who soon made its economy prosper. Apart from the tiny Dutch possessions, Trinidad is the only place in the West Indies where one does not feel stagnation and hopelessness in the air, and this is mainly due to the contributions of the Chinese and the Indians.

The Chinese still control the retail trade in Trinidad, but the crumbs from the rich man's table fall to the indefatigable Syrians, who were the last ones to settle on the little island. They wander from door to door with baskets full of plastic utensils, or stand on street corners, waving colourful pieces of cloth—" Look how strong it is, feel for yourself !"—just like in Aleppo. Where they find a little space between two Chinese shops they open a stand, and many negroes buy from them because they, in contrast to the Chinese, give extensive credit. Their prices are accordingly higher, but then, it is always expensive to be poor.

Anyone who takes a close look at the social structure in Trinidad soon discovers that the ordinary yardstick cannot be used here. One would expect the British rulers to be on the top of the social hierarchy, but many Trinidadians think of them as a kind of parvenu. The real top dogs are the members of the old French families, who have kept their blood surprisingly pure, although a few are a bit dark or have slightly kinky hair.

Having constituted the uppermost class for so long, they are naturally quite exclusive. You seldom see them at " mixed " parties and they stick to their own clubs, some of which seem to be family affairs. In one of them, nearly eighty per cent of the members are called De Verteuiles.

They are also extremely conservative. None of the true bluebloods show up at the annual Bastille day reception given by the French Consul-General. After all, they are royalists!

Not far beneath them are the Chinese. Many of them have become wealthy, owning supermarkets instead of their former little stores, but that is not the only reason why they have been accepted in high society. They have a " good " colour and straight hair—two factors that count nearly as much as money. They are also respected for their oriental tact and politeness. True, it is common knowledge that some members of the older generation still keep concubines and are addicted to opium and gambling, but they cultivate their vices discreetly in their homes or their clubs.

Formerly, the Chinese would go to some little island in

the river deltas when they wanted to indulge their passion for mah-jongg or poker. If a police boat came, the sound of the engine would give them ample warning and time to hide all evidence before the law enforcers jumped ashore. Now it is no longer necessary to be so careful. Gambling is still strictly prohibited, but instead of cash the players now use I.O.U.s which are paid very discreetly.

Occasionally a Chinese will lose everything he owns in a single night, even his house. Then he and his family are permitted to live temporarily at the club and the other members will lend him money for a fresh start.

Although less than ten thousand of Trinidad's population of nearly a million are Chinese, they have left their imprint on the island. Whether negro, Indian or European, you go to a Chinese restaurant when you want a good meal. There are signboards with Chinese characters everywhere, and when Chi-yun and I walked in the narrow, bustling streets of Port of Spain, smiling negroes would often greet her by shouting " Tsao-san," the Cantonese equivalent for " Good morning." But the best illustration of how far the hungry coolies have come was the appointment a few years ago of a Chinese—now Sir Solomon Hochoy—as the first local-born Governor of the island.

After the Chinese come not the Syrians nor the Indians, as one would expect, but the well-to-do blacks. When the negroes many years ago discovered that living off the fat of the land entailed more work than they had reckoned on— especially when Indian competition began pressing down the prices of farm produce—they returned to the cities. The majority were satisfied with working as servants or doing odd jobs in the harbours or oil industry, but a few were more ambitious and sent their children to school. That was the begin-

141

ning of a coloured upper class consisting mainly of white-collar workers, lawyers, doctors and—nowadays—politicians. Having been here relatively so long, they consider themselves superior to the Indians and the Syrians.

It is difficult to say which of the two latter groups has the higher social standing. Many Indians have become wealthy, primarily as owners of taxicabs or cinemas. They have " good " hair, but their skin is deplorably dusky, since they come from the lower castes in India which, generally speaking, are also the darkest.

The Syrians, who also have managed rather well economically, suffer neither from the colour nor from the hair handicap, but most people still look on them as lowly pedlars. Though either Christians or Mohammedans, they are lumped together as " Jewmen." At the bottom of the list is the numerically large coloured lower class which is extremely mixed, although African blood predominates. They are also divided into different " castes." The social climbers usually imitate the whites and sometimes refute their African ancestry.

" I am a true West Indian," I heard one man say. " I have Indian, French, Spanish and Chinese blood in my veins "— leaving out the African, although he was very dark-skinned. Another man admitted that the founder of the local branch of his family was from Africa, but quickly added that he was no slave. No, he had been a chief, who by mistake had been included in a shipload of slaves. As soon as it was discovered that he was of noble blood he was freed, but he chose to remain over here.

At European universities I have twice heard black students from Africa quarrel with black West Indians. When the West Indians under extreme provocation called the Africans " savages," they were overtrumped by the retort, " slave ! "

142

In Western countries a man is often judged by his motor-car. In Trinidad the yardstick is his wife. If she has a relatively light skin, it is whispered that he must be doing well. If, on the other hand, he turns up with a wife who is darker than himself, people will shake their heads pityingly. Poor Jim seems to be on the skids.

This attitude has proved a blessing for the hairdressers, who do a lucrative business straightening out curls for the ladies. For their male customers they can produce a parting in the hair with the aid of a razor. Some even make the skin lighter with the aid of chemicals. When they heard of Europeans smearing themselves with special creams to look sunburned, they shake their heads in amazement—how could anyone wish to be darker?

All this might sound as if racial prejudice is rampant in Trinidad, but the islanders have learned to be considerate towards each other for practical reasons rather than because they subscribe to theories of international brotherhood. Where everyone lives in a glasshouse, it is dangerous to throw stones.

And in this glasshouse a new type of human being is in the making—a type which has preserved many of the better qualities of the races of which it is composed. Its representatives are usually good-looking, with dark, warm skin, slender bodies, a graceful walk and often slightly slanting eyes. When you meet such a person and involuntarily ask yourself where on earth his or her ancestors come from—then you are facing a true Trinidadian!

The negroes have probably contributed the most, and not only because they are numerically superior. It is their music and their happy laughter and spontaneity which greets you everywhere on the island. Many curse them for their laziness, but who says that man has been created primarily to work? Why not let the Chinese and Indians do that?

But the Asians of Trinidad are not as crazy as their diligent ancestors who came here as coolies. They have become bigger, both physically and in their outlook. The Chinese have cut many of the constricting clan ties. They still work hard during the day, but at night one meets them at the capital's excellent cabarets, dancing as hotly as the negroes.

The Indian, who in his homeland is almost devoid of a sense of humour, has learned to take himself a little less seriously. He is still quite frugal, but has begun to put his money in the bank—something that is almost unknown in India where everybody invests in jewellery. The Trinidad Indians do not willingly part with their cash, however. An English banker told us about an Indian cinema owner who put a thousand dollars in the bank. A month later he came and demanded the money. When it was given to him he pushed it back across the counter together with other fat bundles of banknotes. Okay —now he had seen that the bank could be trusted he would like to put some more into his account . . .

The Syrians of Trinidad seem also to have discovered that life can be used for other things than just earning money, and even the local Englishmen carry the white man's burden with much less self-consciousness than they do in other colonies.

Once a year, during carnival week, the whole population melts together into a seething mass. Everybody dances in the streets, and the climax is reached on the last evening in the exclusive Country Club. Dark-hued people do not usually go there, but on this night colour is ignored, and on the stroke of twelve, hundreds of people jump into the swimming pool and splash around with their clothes on—black, white, yellow and all the shades in between. That is when you seem to catch a glimpse of the future Trinidad.

CHAPTER THIRTEEN

THE HOLY MAN

DURING OUR STAY in Trinidad we heard of an Indian holy man called Pundit Sadhu, which means something like " The Wise Sage." His fame as a spiritual guide and nature healer had spread far and wide, and people came to see him from as far away as Brazil.

He lived in the country some twenty miles from Port of Spain and one morning Chi-yun and I went out to visit him. We got off the bus on the main road in a farming area where there were many small peasant holdings. When a young Indian came by on a bicycle we stopped him and asked if he knew where the holy man's house was.

Yes, he replied, alighting. As it happened he lived close to Pundit Sadhu and would show us the way. Indians are about the most candid people in the world, and before long we had learned that the youth's name was Rachid, that he was the son of a farmer and studied law at the University in Port of Spain. At the moment he was at home to celebrate Christmas, which next to the carnival is the most important holiday of the year.

We turned down a dusty side road running beside a meadow. A herd of long-horned Cebu cattle turned their heads slowly to look at us. In their wake stalked stiff-legged herons searching for snails and other titbits among the roots of the grass. Under the bellies of some of the cows, small dark-brown birds darted about, their pointed beaks working like the needle of a sewing machine. They were the Toties, a kind of woodpecker which do their hunting on live animals. It was amusing to see them dangling on the udders of the cows which seemed quite pleased to have their vermin removed in this way.

We walked past some huts which were lying about fifty yards apart, each surrounded by a vegetable garden. Only Indians were living here—one could tell that right away, for the Hindus of Trinidad invariably have some red and white flags waving over the entrance of their homes. The more religious a man is, the more flags he has, Rachid told us.

A delicious smell of curry wafting from one of the houses made me exclaim that I loved Indian food. Then we must lunch with him after our visit to Pundit Sadhu, Rachid immediately said.

Soon we reached his home, an airy and clean hut with two bedrooms and a spartanly furnished dining-room. A total of fourteen people were living here, but only Rachid's mother and grandmother were at home; his father and the children were working in the field. The two women were busy in the kitchen which was a lean-to built over a clay stove. Seeing us they put their palms together and made a gentle dignified bow. After weeks in the company of boisterous and informal negroes I was charmed by this Indian greeting.

Rachid said he would accompany us to the home of Pundit Sadhu, whom he knew well. After walking for a few minutes in the burning sun we reached a tiny hut nearly hidden in a bamboo grove. Over the entrance were a couple of dozen red and white banners—so this must be the home of Pundit

Sadhu. Through the open door we could see a clay idol and some bowls of fruit and some flowers.

I was just going to say that it was most suitable for a holy man to live so modestly when Rachid told us that this was merely Pundit Sadhu's temple. He himself lived in a large and modern villa that rose above the bamboos. In front of the house were a jeep and a shiny new Pontiac. Did they also belong to the holy man? Rachid nodded. Yes, he was very rich; most of the land in this district belonged to him.

We climbed a broad stone staircase and entered a cool reception room. The first thing that caught my eye was a Christmas tree decorated with red and blue electric candles. A young Indian secretary in a smart European suit asked us to sit down in the comfortable easy chairs. He disappeared with my card and a moment later a curtain was pulled aside.

In front of us stood a plump, bespectacled little man in a snow-white gown. His long hair, which was gathered in a knot on the top of his head, contrasted strangely with his thread-like moustache. Slowly he raised his arms and muttered something in a strange tongue. Then he sat down next to us and asked in stilted English why we had come.

I wanted to learn something about the religious practices of the Indians here in Trinidad, I replied. Again he raised his arms.

" God is truth, and the truth is God," he declared. I asked which Indian god was most popular on the island—Vishnu or Krishna his flute-playing re-incarnation, or Ganesh, the gay god with the head of an elephant?

" All and none," the sage replied enigmatically. " For clean living men all ways lead to Brahma, otherwise none."

What did he mean by clean living? You should not be

greedy, not eat meat and you should meditate, he replied, placing his hands on his folded knees and closing his eyes. He would sit like this by the hour, he assured us.

Again he began to mutter something incomprehensible, but suddenly I recognized some of the words. He was not speaking Hindi as I had thought—he was merely reciting the rivers of India without a pause between the names!

I made a few more attempts to learn something more concrete, but each time I asked a question I would get a reply which could mean anything—God was good, evil was bad, and so on. He would not tell me how many patients he had nor how he treated them—he just followed the instructions of God and, as everybody knows, the ways of the Lord are unfathomable.

Was he a Brahmin? Yes, very much so! He had acquired his learning partly from ancient Indian writings, partly from God. But wasn't it unusual for a Brahmin to celebrate the birthday of Christ? I asked, glancing at the Christmas tree. No, every one did in Trinidad. God was one, Indusgangesbrahmaputra . . .

When we were outside on the road again, I drew a deep breath and asked Rachid if he knew anything about Pundit Sadhu's background. Yes, he could still remember how the man had come to this district eight or nine years ago. In those days he had been a poor labourer with an ordinary Indian name, and he ate meat like everybody else, and only after being here for a couple of years did he begin to take patients.

" Then he's just a quack!" I exclaimed indignantly, but Rachid did not agree. Some of his medicaments were made from roots and herbs, but he also used modern medicine prescribed for him by a young Indian doctor who had studied at Kingston.

In any case he was not a real Brahmin, I continued. Rachid shrugged his shoulders. It turned out that although Rachid's family had been in the West Indies for only three generations he knew nothing about how the priestly caste had oppressed the poor in India for thousands of years, nor even that the people in his motherland were divided into strictly segregated social groups.

" It is a good thing it isn't like that here," was all he said when I told him about it. How fortunate it was that the immigrants had left the caste system behind them in the old world, I thought.

We went out into the fields to find his father and call him home for lunch. On the way, Rachid told us that the Indians of Trinidad did not take religion too seriously. His father was a Mohammedan, his mother a Hindu and his old grandmother, who was a widow, was a member of the Catholic church. Which church did he himself belong to?

" I haven't decided yet," he replied with a smile. Like most of the Indians, he went to the religious festivals of both the Mohammedans and the Hindus. There would be a short sermon, usually by a lay preacher, followed by a sumptuous meal. Some of the negroes of the district went too. They were Catholics, but that did not matter. Many of them spoke a little Hindi and as a child Rachid had hardly known that there was a difference between Indians and negroes.

All this indicated an unusual degree of tolerance, I said, but Rachid found it quite natural. All the religions were nearly alike, apart from the rules about eating and fasting, and those were only observed by the old people. In his family they ate everything . . .

We had come to a small river and suddenly the water became alive as if a flock of boys had started to play ducks and drakes. It was a school of " big-eyes," as they are called in Trinidad—a transparent, tadpole-like creature, half fish, half insect. They had fled as soon as they discovered us, but when we had been standing stock still for a few minutes they slowly returned. All we could see of them were round eyes which seemed to be watching us steadily as they cruised back and forth on the surface of the water. As soon as we waded out into the water they disappeared again, leaving long ripples behind them.

Close to the brook we found Rachid's father, a bony, slightly hunched man, whose slender hands did not seem to belong to a farmer. He was busy weeding a vegetable bed aided by five of his bigger children. They were almost through when we came, and in single file we set out for home along the narrow path.

How much land did they have? Thirty acres, Rachid's father replied, but only eight belonged to him. The rest he rented at slightly over five pounds a year per acre. None of his fields was ever allowed to lie fallow. In the spring he grew rice and after that had been harvested he could raise two crops of vegetables during the rest of the year. This was only possible because the whole family lent a hand, however. He could hire a negro day labourer for about a shilling an hour, but the negroes had little feeling for agriculture and would often weed out the wrong plants, so that virtually all the farmers in Trinidad were Indians.

Back home in the little dining-room the table had been set for only four. Rachid's mother and grandmother would not hear of joining us. Who would then serve the food?

In honour of us they had slaughtered a chicken which was served with a delicious curry sauce that nearly made our hair stand on end. Rachid used knife and fork, but his father used his fingers in Indian fashion. In a few years no one would eat this way any more, he said. The young people were ashamed of doing it.

"Look!" Chi-yun pointed out of the window. She had spotted a tiny, bright green humming bird which seemed to be standing stock-still in the air; its wings were moving so fast that one could only see a blur and it had its head inside a flower. These little birds are found only in the Western world, where in the summer they go as far north as the snow boundary in Alaska. I had read that they can fly at a speed of nearly eighty miles an hour, and when the bird left the flower a moment later, I quite believed this. Whoosh! and it was gone!

During the meal Rachid told us that next year he would be going to London to complete his studies. With an English diploma in his pocket he would be made. We were of course surprised to hear that a simple farmer could afford to let his son study abroad, but that was possible only because the whole family worked hard and lived frugally.

"My elder brother is also studying in England," Rachid added. "He has already been there for two years. He is going to be a doctor." He showed us a picture of a young man who looked exactly like himself. The father looked away. The elder brother had caused them great sorrow by marrying an English woman, Rachid explained in a low voice.

But was that really such a bad thing to do? Yes—not so much because she belonged to another race; that mattered little in Trinidad where so many were of mixed blood. But Europeans had expensive habits. They had to have a fine house and a motor-car. How could his brother help the family when he had an English wife to support?

The parents did not want to run the same risk with Rachid,

so he had to marry before he left. They had already found a suitable wife for him.

The afternoon bus was passing by soon, so we had to take leave of the family. Rachid accompanied us to the main road. When we were waiting at the bus stop, Chi-yun asked him if he did not mind that his parents had chosen his bride for him.

" No," he replied, " I think that's the best way."

Some of the traditions of Asia had survived the transplantation to the new world, I thought, and then the bus came.

CHAPTER FOURTEEN

CHRISTMAS IN SHANTY TOWN

WHEN WE HAD nearly reached the end of the long row of hovels I stopped. What on earth was this? There was no mistaking the little veranda with the potted plants on the railing, but I would have sworn that the hut had been a dirty grey the last time I had seen it. Now it was shining with red and light-green paint!

" I think it was here," I said hesitatingly to Chi-yun. For a moment we listened to the cacophony coming out through the open door. Laughter intermingled with noisy chatter, the crying of a child, and someone beating a drum.

Then a face appeared at the window. The voices became silent, the drumbeats died out, and the child stopped crying. In the sudden stillness we could again hear the church bells of Port of Spain which had chimed since dawn, for it was Christmas morning.

" Merry Christmas—come on inside!" A tall negress in a white dress appeared in the doorway. It was Elvira, whom I had met some days ago while taking a walk in the slum district. Then she had been in the midst of her annual Christmas cleaning and was wearing a soiled slip, sitting in front of the house, busily engaged in staining a chair. We had chatted for a while, and when she heard that I was interested in the life of

153

the negroes in Trinidad, she had invited me to her Christmas party. With my wife, she had added when I told her that I was married.

Inside, too, the hut was almost unrecognizable. It smelled of varnish and paint and newly-washed curtains, and all the shelves were lined with coloured paper. About a dozen dark faces looked searchingly at us. The women, who like Elvira were dressed in white, occupied the three chairs and the sofa.

The men sat on the floor, each holding a glass, and half-naked children were crawling wherever they could find the space.

For several minutes there was a watchful silence, but when the hip-flask of rum which I had brought along had gone round twice, their shyness began to disappear. The women wanted to be urged—just a tiny sip for your sake, they said coyly; but the men grinningly filled the ladies' glasses to the brim and said, " Down the hatch, sister !"

I noticed that they hardly ever finished their drinks completely, but poured the last few drops on to the floor or out of the window. When I asked why, they replied that they had always done so. I wondered whether it was an old custom brought over from Africa. There one can still see people pour the last of a drink on the earth for the gods.

Elvira told us that she had lived for five years in Shanty Town and liked it. Of course it was troublesome to have to fetch your water from the public pump, but you were left in peace by the police—they pretended that this section of town did not exist.

Some of the inhabitants of Shanty Town were nice people, she continued. For instance, the last hut on this road belonged to an Indian who worked for the transport department. He did not want to pay the exorbitant rents in town so, like the others here, he had built his own house.

Soon there would be no more Shanty Town, however, as it was scheduled to be pulled down in six months' time. Where were they going to live then? The authorities were building fine new houses for them in another part of the town, Elvira replied. She would never get to live there though, nor would many of the others.

Why not? She explained that most of the houses in Shanty Town had already been bought by wealthy people from town who thus acquired the right to the reasonably-priced new houses. She herself had been paid several times the value of her hut. Was she sorry that she would never get to live in one of the new houses? Not really—there had never been a chance of her doing so anyway, since the authorities were charging a down payment of six hundred dollars. Hardly anyone here could raise that much. What would they do when they were forced to move? She shrugged her shoulders. Build a new Shanty Town somewhere else she supposed . . .

" Hey—here comes the Killer!" someone shouted as another guest entered. The man who went under this sinister nickname was a calypso singer, a plump little fellow, nearly toothless and with a guitar under his arm. Behind him, a little unsteady on his feet, came a man in shorts, undershirt—and rubber boots.

The first thing he did was to pull a cutlass out of a boot and put it in a corner of the room. I then noticed that the other guests had already deposited their knives at the same spot. One did not carry weapons when among friends, but after dark they could be useful in the unlit streets of Shanty Town, where there were many toughs and robbers who would attack peaceful folk, Elvira said.

Most acts of violence in Trinidad are committed with the cutlass, and curiously enough, mainly by Indians. Their partiality for this weapon probably goes back to the time when they worked on the plantations and always carried one.

Its use is not restricted to fights and agriculture. If an Indian becomes irritated about something or other—for instance if his wife has not cleaned his rice thoroughly of small stones—he may resort to the cutlass. Hardly a day passes without several bloody cutlass dramas, but they are seldom fatal. Usually the opponents just slash each other on the thigh or shoulder. The punishment for doing so is comparatively mild, perhaps because this offence is so common. Generally speaking, the fine for a single slash is the same as for a parking offence . . .

The Killer greeted the other guests affably, but when his glance fell on me he revealed his pink gums in an insolent smile.

" Ah-ha, and to what do we owe the honour of such a special visit?" he drawled. I was on the point of answering that I liked the company, but his next remark silenced me.

" White folks never come here without a purpose," he continued. " I see that the gentleman has brought his camera along, so I suppose he wants to take pictures of the black people's Christmas celebration?"

He snarled the last words, and the truth in them made me wince. My expression must have told him that it was a bull's-eye, for he added triumphantly, " Then let him pay for it! He probably has lots of money. Why should we give him something for nothing? They never do . . ."

"You talk too much, Killer," someone interrupted. " I think you missed your vocation in life. You should have been a preacher instead!"

They all burst out laughing, and the little musician also had difficulty in keeping a straight face. " Yes—let's have a song instead of all this preachifying," another one put in.

" Okay, okay—the majority wins!" The Killer nodded good-naturedly. " After all, we're democratic here in Trinidad." He strummed his guitar, put his foot on the edge of a chair and began to sing in a deep, pleasant voice :

> *" In the world I know there are millions of whites*
> *Who appreciate the coloured man's rights,*
> *And have a desire and willingness*
> *To aid in his pursuit of happiness.*
> *A white man could love a negro to the core*
> *As a brother—but not as a brother-in-law,*
> *So these mixed marriages in my opinion*
> *Is the cause of all this racial discrimination."*

They laughed and clapped their hands, and the next song also made a hit. It was about England's attempt to amalgamate its nine West Indian dependencies under a single federated government. Judging by the statements of British politicians, this was to be done primarily for the sake of the natives, but The Killer had a different idea. After having reaped a golden harvest during slave times. England now wanted to get rid of the poverty-stricken little islands on which it was losing money, so it tried to hand the responsibility to the two biggest and richest of the islands, Trinidad and Jamaica.

" *But Whitehall won't get away with dat!*" came the refrain after each verse. (Shortly afterwards Jamaica and then Trinidad left the Federation and were promised their independence in the near future. The smaller islands will probably remain in a federation which will be closely tied to England. Without aid from Britain in the form of an over-price for sugar, most of the islands could not manage.)

" Bravo, bravo!" they shouted at the end of the song. " Come on, Killer—give it to them!"

He emptied his glass and began to sing again. I think he improvised many of the songs, for several of those present were described, though in such anatomical detail that they are unfortunately unfit to print.

Several began to dance, not in couples, but each one by himself, like the West Africans. First they hummed, but soon they were singing at the top of their voices, with closed eyes, the lower parts of their bodies working like pistons. The women unbuttoned their dresses and the men took off their shirts and long trousers and danced in their shorts. When a dish of boiled ham was brought in, they grabbed a handful in passing, stuffed it into their mouths and washed it down with more rum.

Elvira, who was sitting between Chi-yun and me, pointed to a broad-shouldered fellow. I had already noticed him, for he wore a couple of rings on each of his thick fingers. That was her husband, she said. He was foreman of a gang who were building a road through the swamps west of Port of Spain—a government project aimed chiefly at relieving un-employment among the negroes. He used to be a bad boy, she said—begged and stole, but after he got a steady job there was no need for it any more. Now he earned nearly twenty pounds a month and could afford to be respectable. He was a good, steady man, apart from the fact that he drank too much rum once in a while, but then nearly everyone did.

How long had they been married? They were not mar-ried, Elvira replied—hardly any people were here in Shanty

Town. They just lived together. Why get married? It cost money and it was not good for a man to get so much power over a woman. It went to his head and made him treat her badly.

Elvira had been a waitress at a nightclub in town from the time she was sixteen. Since then she had had one baby a year, all by different men. This she told us as if it were the most natural thing in the world.

As I listened to her, my thoughts went back to something I had often speculated about during my trip through the West Indies, and especially since my arrival in Trinidad. Why have the negroes been practically standing still since they were freed a century and a half ago?

Of course, it can be said that they started out with a handicap. The great majority of them could neither read nor write —but neither could the Chinese and the Indians when they came to Trinidad as ignorant coolies, and they have worked themselves to the top just the same.

Several times I had come close to drawing the conclusion that the negroes were poorer human material than the other racial groups, but Elvira's words made me wonder whether there was not another explanation to their backwardness. During the time of slavery, the plantation owners did their best to eradicate all family feeling among the negroes. They were welcome to have children—the more the better—but the parents were not allowed to live together. The offspring belonged to the whites—the slaves could not own anything.

The negroes accepted this, and the abolition of slavery did nothing to change their attitude. They had never felt any responsibility towards the children they put into this world, and they still don't. That is why the West Indian islands are full of half-wild children who are never sent to school. A blow

if they get in the way of the grown-ups is about the extent
of their education.

No wonder I had often felt that the West Indian negroes
lacked the natural dignity of the African negroes. They had
grown up without traditions, without any discipline. Perhaps
the curse of slavery must be passed on through seven generations . . .

The rum flowed freely and the dancing was becoming
wild when Chi-yun and I left towards noon. The Killer had
just started a new song—something about people saying that
he stank, but that was impossible, for he was too lazy to
sweat. He was also accused of being an idler, but that too
was a misunderstanding, for " *I'm too lazy to be lazy . . .*"

That was the last we heard before we started out on the
dusty road back to Port of Spain.

CHAPTER FIFTEEN

RED JANET

OUR JOURNEY ENDED in British Guiana, the old sugar colony on the South American continent, north of the mouth of the Amazon. When we stepped ashore at the capital after a two-day voyage from Trinidad, we expected to find one of the usual primitive towns of the Caribbean, only hotter, for we were much further south now. Georgetown had several happy surprises in store for us, however. It faces the sea, which all the year round sends a cool breeze over the low-lying coast. Even when the sun is directly overhead the temperature is no higher than it is on a hot summer's day back home.

The town turned out to be an oasis in the architectural desert of the Caribbean area, and for this we can thank the Dutch. It was they who colonized the Guiana coast, and some of the beautiful and spacious wooden houses which they built are still standing—among them the largest wooden church in the world. Some districts have a faint flavour of old Holland, only there is more space between the buildings than in the crowded mother country. The broad boulevards are shaded by gnarled trees which were also planted by the far-sighted Dutch.

Without them, Georgetown and the other Guianese cities would hardly exist, for when the first whites came here the coast was nothing but a mangrove swamp. A few expeditions penetrated into the interior, where it was believed that the fabulous Eldorado was hidden. Only a few trembling derelicts returned to tell about endless rain forests and impassable mountains where the fever lay in wait for those who were not eaten by cannibals or wild animals.

Sir Walter Raleigh, who also went there, called Guiana " . . . a land that hath not yet lost its maidenhead." For a while it looked as if it might be permitted to keep it, for when the dreams of finding gold had been shattered, the Europeans set sail for more promising coasts.

But then a group of men from the Low Countries came. The swamps did not discourage them—that was an enemy they knew well at home. They imported negro slaves and set them to work building dikes and sluices and digging canals. When windmills had pumped out the muddy brackish water into the sea, they planted sugar cane. One could almost see the green plants shoot out of the earth, and soon the gold of the New World streamed via Europe into the pockets of the diligent settlers.

Towards the close of the seventeenth century the dikes had been extended until they protected a fertile coastal strip more than six hundred miles in length. Of course the Dutch were not permitted to keep so rich a country for themselves. The French annexed eastern Guiana, and at the beginning of the nineteenth century, the British conquered the north-western part.

After the abolition of slavery, the leaders of the three colonies had to look around for labour, for here too the negroes went on an extended holiday, which has not really terminated as yet. The Dutch imported Javanese from the East Indies, the English brought in coolies from China and India, and the

162

French, convicts from home, so it became a motley population.

The high mountains and deep forests isolated the area from the independence movement which broke the Spanish and Portuguese yoke in the New World. British, Dutch and French Guiana, which cover nearly twice the area of their mother countries, remained the only colonies in South America.

For a long time they were plagued by a malignant malaria which seemed to grow worse as the years went by. The mortality as a result of the deadly fever was so high that the population of the three Guianas for years remained at 800,000, although the birthrate was exceptionally high. Sometimes more than half the workers at the big plantations were on the sick-list, and in some places the fields were taken over by the jungle because it was impossible to get enough people on their feet to weed them.

But towards the end of the Second World War, new life was suddenly blown into the stagnating colonies. That was due to the new insecticide D.D.T., which the Americans brought with them wherever they fought or had bases. In British Guiana a great campaign was started against the death-bringing mosquitoes. It gave quicker results than anyone had dared to hope.

" It was as if the whole people rose after a long sickness," was how an old resident of Georgetown described it to us.

A wave of energy and *joie de vivre* swept the land, but the large coloured population found itself bound and gagged by an antiquated colonial system. There were no political parties —what would have been the use of them when all decisions were made by English officials? The only Union was a puppet organization, founded and financed by the large sugar companies. They owned around four-fifths of the cultivated coastal strip, as well as the Press, all the department stores and most of the ships that sailed to British Guiana. Thanks to their size and enormous wealth, these companies dominated the English administration.

No one expected that the young Indian dentist, who in the late forties returned to British Guiana after completing his studies in the United States, would dare to challenge this monopolistic concentration of power. His mild, rather indecisive manner did not seem suited for a political career, and if he had been single, it is quite possible that he would have contented himself with setting up a practice in Georgetown and tending the teeth of the upper classes.

But Cheddi Jagan was accompanied by his bride, an energetic American girl who burned with eagerness to reform her husband's country. It is said that Janet Jagan has contributed more than whisky to cause high blood pressure among the whites in the colony. This may be an exaggeration, but it is certain that almost from the very day when " Red Janet " set foot in British Guiana, the local upper class has been exposed to one shock after another.

The thin, bespectacled American girl with the cold smile made her entry into the colony wearing a sari, which in itself was enough to make tongues wag. The Indians, who had come out as indentured labourers, were a despised group in British Guiana. It was bad enough for a white woman to marry one of them, but to emphasize her shamelessness by wearing Indian clothes—that was a scandal!

It was customary to invite well-mannered European women of mixed marriages to a party once in a while, but the " better circles " in the colony decided to reject any advances made by the American upstart. Janet and Cheddi made matters worse by not even giving the whites an opportunity to show their contempt. They only sought the company of " coloured " people or of the few liberal Europeans—who of course were accused of being Communists. After a short stay in the capital, the young couple went to visit Cheddi's father, who was a driver on a plantation.

Janet's University days had approximately coincided with the honeymoon period between Roosevelt and Stalin during the last war. She had been strongly influenced by Russian ideas and had been one of the leaders of a Communistic youth organization at her University. Some believe that she agreed to marry Cheddi primarily to try her hand as a revolutionary in his country. This may be true, but from the moment she saw the home in which her husband had grown up together with eight sisters and brothers, she was undoubtedly motivated also by sympathy for the poor of Guiana.

It must have shocked the young girl, who came from a middle-class home in Chicago, to see the rows upon rows of wretched huts in which the plantation workers lived. Eight people would often sleep in a small room, and twenty-odd families had to fetch water from the same pump and share an old-fashioned toilet. The workers were not permitted to build their own houses outside the plantations nor to grow vegetables on the large tracts of land which belonged to the plantations, but which were not used. The aim was to make the workers completely dependent on their employers.

As a result of this policy, there is an acute shortage of agricultural land in the inhabited areas, although more than ninety-nine per cent of the country is still a wilderness. Only the large companies have the capital necessary for clearing the jungle.

The young couple had not been very long in British Guiana before there were rumours of suspicious happenings at the plantations. The workers began leaving the old Union, which was still controlled by the plantation owners. Instead, they joined a new and aggressive Union founded by Cheddi Jagan. He and his wife encouraged them to demand higher wages and better living conditions.

About this time a cloudburst caused a severe flood. For weeks, the workers at one of the largest plantations waded around in water up to their knees, and toads and mud came out of the public pumps. All the workers turned up when the new Union called a meeting to protest against these conditions. Enthusiastically they voted for Cheddi's resolution demanding the company to postpone the draining of the cane fields until the water had been pumped away from the area where the workers lived. They also asked for clean drinking water.

After the meeting Cheddi Jagan went to the plantation manager to hand him the resolution. When he had listened for a while to the Indian, he looked coldly at him and said: " If you don't get off the premises at once I shall send for the police."

This episode made Jagan realize that peaceful means would not be sufficient if he wanted to do something for the poor. From that day on, the members of his Union used force in their struggle with their employers. Hardly had one strike been settled before the next one began. The police were repeatedly used against the workers, who retaliated by beating up the managers.

Cheddi, who meanwhile had been elected to represent the plantation workers in a newly-established legislative council, now decided to start his own party. The " People's Progressive Party," as he called it, was an immediate success. Both the Indians and the negroes, who were about equal in number, were attracted by the party's programme which clearly bore the imprint of Janet. She was generous with glowing promises, and some sections were taken almost word for word from Communist manifestos.

" The struggle between the exploiters and the exploited is the only one that really matters in British Guiana today," Cheddi Jagan declared in his maiden speech. He asked for " tolerable living conditions " for the masses and immediate independence.

London refused to go as far as that, but as a result of the growing demand for independence, the colony was granted in 1953 a constitution which complied with many of Jagan's demands. The English Governor had to share the reins with a Guianese government elected by the people.

In the election that followed, the " P.P.P.", as Jagan's party is called, captured nearly eighty per cent of the votes and Janet and Cheddi took over as heads of a leftist government.

Six months later the Governor used his veto power to suspend the constitution and dismiss the new government. As a result of its policy, chaos threatened to engulf the colony, he declared. He further accused Jagan of harbouring plans to crush democracy in British Guiana and introduce a Communist dictatorship. To prevent this, British troops were flown to the colony.

Later, an investigation showed that these charges were largely unfounded. It was true that Cheddi, spurred by Janet, had led the colony far out to the left. Among other things, they had ordered the printing of new school books praising the Soviet Union, and the government had sided with the new Union in its struggle with the sugar companies. It is not unlikely that Jagan's rule would have led to chaos had it been permitted to run its devious course, for several members of the new government were inexperienced theorists, others were simply incompetent and corrupt.

But the Governor had cried thief before Jagan had stolen. There was no proof that he had planned to establish himself as a dictator, nor had he done anything unconstitutional.

The Governor and the sugar companies had won a temporary victory, but their attempts to set the clock back undoubtedly harmed their cause in the long run. Jagan could not be silenced, and now his attraction was enhanced by the halo of martyrdom. In 1957, when elections were held for a new government, which was however to have only limited powers, both he and his wife were candidates. The great majority voted for the young couple.

Janet became Minister of Public Health, Labour and Housing, Cheddi, Minister of Trade and Industry. The lethargic English administrators in their departments did not get much peace during the next few years. Janet hectored them unmercifully until all the towns and larger villages had been supplied with clean drinking water. She also saw to it that the government built thousands of small, comfortable bungalows which were rented out cheaply to the lower classes. The public health service was brought up to date and the plantations were forced to agree to a minimum wage of about twelve shillings a day. Under Cheddi's leadership, the government encouraged small industries, thus indirectly aiding the many unemployed in the colony.

In 1961, when London for the second time decided to hand over full powers to a government elected by the Guianese people, Cheddi and Janet were more popular than ever. Before the election, however, something happened which was to upset Jagan's career considerably. His closest associate, a leftist negro by the name of Burnham, left him and founded his

own party. There were no ideological differences between the
two men. The negro simply saw a chance of getting power
and could not resist the temptation.

The P.P.P. was split wide open. All the negroes in the
colony, regardless of their political inclinations, immediately
went to the support of their racial brother. The Indians—
even ultra-conservatives who had protested vehemently against
the P.P.P.'s "Bolshevism"—joined up behind Jagan. The
whites and many of the Chinese formed a third party under
a demagogic Portuguese brewer.

The ensuing election campaign was in many ways remini-
scent of a circus performance. The P.P.P., anxious to prove
that it was above racial issues, nominated a negro as its candidate in an almost purely Indian district on the outskirts of
Georgetown. His name was Lawrence Mann, but to be on the
safe side he temporarily changed it to Lalmansingh, the Indian
equivalent of Jones, and worshipped in a Hindu temple wearing Indian clothes. When a Portuguese, who was a candidate
in Burnham's party, was greeted with anti-European slogans
at a rally, he is said to have calmed down the audience by
yelling: "My skin may be white, but my heart is
black!"

A discussion on the radio was arranged so that the three
party leaders could elucidate their plans for the colony's
economic future. Burnham, who clearly had no plans, parried
Jagan's embarrassing questions by shouting: "Why should
I reply? If I do you'll steal my ideas!"

Some began to wonder whether the colony was ready for
self-government.

Jagan won a narrow victory, but Burnham and the brewer
now joined forces and started a campaign of hatred against
him, supported by the Press. They called him a Bolshevik in

one breath and in the next accused him of planning to introduce a dictatorship of the Indians in British Guiana.

Negroes and Indians, who until then had been living together in peace, began to eye each other with suspicion. Were
all these ugly accusations true? The awakening nationalism,
which alone could make British Guiana into a nation, found a
powerful rival in racial loyalties.

Burnham and the Portuguese brewer fanned the smouldering embers. Did they realize that by weakening Jagan's pres-
tige they also undermined the respect for representative government and for authority altogether? Before long, bloody
fights between blacks and browns became the order of the
day.

The campaign of hatred ended with an explosion in Georgetown in the spring of 1962. The population of the capital
consists mainly of negroes—perhaps that is why it did not turn
into a racial struggle, but rather a blind blow against the
authorities.

A black mob, which had been aroused against an unpopular tax law, ran amok. It broke into shops, looted them and
set them on fire. Large sections of the business area were in
flames and many people killed before Jagan finally went to
the Governor. It must have been humiliating for him, the
anti-colonial socialist, to ask his old enemy, the representative
of England's power, for troops to be used against the people.
But there was no other way out . . .

When Chi-yun and I came to Georgetown, " Red Janet "
was away on a tour behind the Iron Curtain, but we succeeded in getting an interview with Cheddi Jagan. Tired and
seemingly depressed, the forty-two-year-old Prime Minister sat
behind his desk. He was grey at the temples and had deep
wrinkles in his forehead. For nearly a year he had been in

power, and what had he achieved during this period?

About fifty thousand acres of land had been reclaimed from the jungle and turned into smallholdings. A couple of dozen new schools had been built and some of the few existing roads had been paved. But none of the sweeping social reforms which he and Janet had dreamed of had been realized. How could they, when the people were divided against themselves and his enemies were using every opportunity to trip him?

He had not abandoned his plans, however, only postponed them. The young people in the Party were still being indoctrinated with Communistic ideas, and some were sent to Cuba to learn from Castro's revolution.

Though no one to date has received a clear-cut answer, every visiting journalist invariably asks Jagan whether he is a Communist. That I did not do so was because he stole a march on me.

"I am a Marxist," he said. "I believe that a planned economy is the best way to solve the problems of the underdeveloped countries."

That did not mean that he intended to introduce dictatorship. Like so many leftist intellectuals in the underdeveloped countries, he preferred, if possible, to carry out social reforms with democratic methods. He believed in democracy, he said, but not in capitalism.

What about President Kennedy's Alliance for Progress, which proposed to spend some twenty million dollars in Latin America during the next decade or two?

It was an inspiring gesture, but the plan seemed to be a move in the cold war which British Guiana did not want to be dragged into. He needed a loan badly, for lately there had been a flight of capital from the country, but he wanted a loan without political strings attached—and he would accept it from anyone.

How many of the billions of dollars which the United States had poured into Latin America since the last war had not ended in Swiss banks, in the private accounts of reactionary politicians? Jagan asked. No, loans would not do the trick until the social structure had been changed in most of the underdeveloped countries. Underneath a surface of modernity you often found a feudal structure which permitted a few to exploit the many.

His party wanted to do away with all such exploitation. The Guianese no longer wanted to have their fate decided by foreign capitalists whose sole aim was to make high profits and who invested only in the production of raw materials, never in industries.

If the underdeveloped countries did not become masters of their own house, they were doomed to become poorer and poorer in relation to the West, Jagan continued. As it was, two-thirds of the income of the world went to one-fifth of its population, the fifth which lives in the industrialized countries. If nothing is done, the abyss will widen, because the terms of trade are changing steadily in favour of the well-to-do nations. Thus, today the Guianese need forty per cent more sugar to import the same amount of industrial goods and foodstuffs as in 1947.

"We are tired of being poor stepchildren," Jagan concluded. Chi-yun and I remembered his words long after we had left, for they seemed to be spoken on behalf of the entire under-developed—the coloured—world.

INDEX

173